Mindset, Marketing & Money

Vol 1

Successful Entrepreneurs
Share Their 3 Biggest Secrets
About Business & Online
Success

Nicola Cairncross

FREE GIFTS FOR READERS OF THIS BOOK

If you would like download several free gifts just visit our website and click the About You links in the top menu.

Don't forget to download the free App to keep up to date!

NicolaCairncross.com/app

If you would like Nicola to mentor you on how to start an online business OR how to market your existing business better online just visit NicolaCairncross.com and download one of our free gifts and we'll send you more info about the "Inner Circle" mentoring programme.

CONTENTS

FREE GIFTS FOR READERS OF THIS BOOK

CONTENTS

DEDICATION

ACKNOWLEDGMENTS

1. JAMES SCHRAMKO

2. JENI HOTT

3. DAN NORRIS

4. RICH SCHEFREN

5. Margaret Wright

6. RYAN LEVESQUE

ABOUT THE AUTHOR

OTHER BOOKS BY NICOLA
    "The Business Success Factory"
    "The Money Gym: The Ultimate Wealth Workout (2nd edition)"
    "How To Market ANY Business Online"
    "The Science Of Getting Rich Online"

FREE GIFTS FOR READERS OF THIS BOOK

DEDICATION

Everything I do, I do for my gorgeous children (all grown up now!) Phoebe & Nelson, being your Mum is the best thing that ever happened to me.

In loving memory of

Steve G. Watson

ACKNOWLEDGMENTS

I would like to thank the amazing entrepreneurs who gave up an hour of their precious time to share their secrets with me for the podcast and this book.

I also want to acknowledge you, the entrepreneur reading this book, for your dedication to improving your mind and entrepreneurial skills.

Remember, even if you lost everything, you still have your mind and the knowledge contained within, so you are always richer than most!

1. JAMES SCHRAMKO

Nicola: Today I'm delighted to be joined by James Schramko from SuperFastBusiness.com. James is proof positive that you can take solid business profit ideas and turn then into a powerful online business. Leaving the safety of a 300,000 dollar a year general management role, running a Mercedes Benz dealership in Sydney, James starts his online career with just one affiliate product.

With a $49.25 commission per sale. James turned that into a 6 figure a year online business and then quickly developed his own business well past the million dollar mark. A few years later he generates a 7 figure profit from his online coaching website in traffic businesses. Importantly, James is a master of the core elements that you can tap into quickly; traffic, conversions, and leverage. Plus, I doubt you'll find a more approachable marketer on the planet. Welcome to the call, James.

James: Thanks Nicola, I appreciate you having me on the show.

Nicola :I was just listening to some of your, well, I listen to your Super Fast business podcast anyway, but I was listening to your one with Clay Collins last night, and I want to thank you finally explaining in ways I could understand, what lead links are all about.

James: It's one of my curiosities, is to take these brand names and complex and terms and get behind what they actually are and simplify them so that I can understand them and then that other people can understand them as well.

Nicola : It's an awesome business model, isn't it? Every time I use it I think, "Blimey, they've really created something here that you just can't do without once you start using it."

James: I think that's one of the secrets, it's to solve problems and put it on a recurring payment program.

Nicola : They've done that really well. If you had to ask me which of my tools I need and I can't do without, it would be Lead Pages nowadays, that's for sure. Let's hear about your business. I'm particularly interested in what makes people become the entrepreneurs they are today. I see that you were doing really really well in a job. Tell me about your background and where you grew up and what kind of family you grew up in and how you became the Mercedes Benz success dealership you were, and then what made you become an entrepreneur after that?

James: I think I was an entrepreneur before that, if I look back. I grew up, I just had one sister, I had nice parents. We grew up in a very expensive and exclusive suburb of Sydney. I went to an expensive private school. For all intensive purposes, we were a very wealthy and fortunate family. My parents are really grounded, having, my dad grew up reasonably poor and my mom has always worked for charities and organizations.

We used to go out on tours around the state to poorer areas and I was fully aware that I was in a privileged upbringing. After school, which I didn't do so well at, I must admit, I started a course for about the only thing that I qualified for which was an accounting course at a technology university that we had here. It's not quite a university, it's more of a an accredited school.

I got sick, so I pulled out. I worked in all sorts of jobs for a year. I labored, I worked in [inaudible 00:05:04], I did some Fridays at an accounting firm. Then I started the next year. Another half a year after that my parents lost all their money, and we had to move out of the fancy home. I realized at that point that we were no longer rich and I had to go and get a job. My first first full time job, which paid about $18,500 a year in 1991. It was about half what all my mates we on.

That was a debt collection, of all things, which is a good thing to do when there's a recession. I learned plenty of things there, but I also realized, even at that point, at 20 years old, I'd been lucky enough to have exposed to some good practices from my grandparents, one of whom was a timber broker, and he used to buy and sell timber on the telephone. Having worked with him part time, I had superior telephone skills to my peers. Also, I was lucky enough when I was just 12 years old to read a selling book.

It was the only book available at an airport, which was a midnight flight. I didn't even know what selling was and I bought it and read it, and picked up a lot of the ideas from it without really understanding it so much. I had some idea that this selling thing was useful. Tom Hopkins talks about it being one of the best careers you could have that's an unlimited income.

In between, I'd done all these part time jobs, which had helped me learn more about people and communications. Things like my lawn mowing round taught me a lot about the psychology of pricing things. Where a rich family will pay a lot more, even for a small lawn to be mowed than a budget conscious family who had a large area, they might want to pay a lot less. I could tell there were a lot of clues; the car they were driving, the clothes they were wearing, the way that they approached the negotiations would often indicate to me where I should be pricing the job.

Then I learned other things like referral marketing. When I'd mow the lawn at one house, I'd knock on the door of all the neighbors and say, "Hey, listen I'm just mowing the lawn next door, would you like me to do yours as well for 20 bucks?" Because they'd already heard the lawn mower and they'd already gone through that process of, "Oh, I've got to mow our lawn, it's getting long, and I don't want to do it." It was like this gift from heaven.

Some guy at the door wants to mow my lawn for 20 bucks. I ended up having a whole street.

At this time I learned another valuable lesson, and that is that if you have all of your eggs in one basket, it's easier for someone to step on it. A develop bought that block and knocked down all the houses. I lost all my clients in one go.

Nicola : No compensation for you.

James: I learned that I shouldn't be single source dependent.

Nicola : You've really absorbed a lot of lessons very quickly there, haven't you? Were you where you were absorbing, or is it only in hindsight that you realized that you picked it all up?

James: I often reflect on how I've engineered the situation that I have now. I think when you're reading one book or you listen to one podcast, you're only ever getting the tip of the iceberg. There's so much. If you think about it, in 40 years, you get exposed to a lot of stuff. So many lessons, every single day there's lessons. If you add them all up, what you have now is the grand sum total of everything you've learned, everything you've applied and all the actions you've taken and the behaviors you've acquired. Everything you have right now is the grand sum total of that. There's a few principles along the way that have helped me refine that.

One of the things that stood out for me was this kaizen principle of never ending improvement. It's a Japanese principle, but it's always looking to improve and optimize what you have. I think there's no greater place to do that than your brain. The way that you think can be optimized and it can continually deliver better situations for you when you clean up the way that you think compared to the way that most people think.

The way that most people think is taught to us at schools and by parents, so if I were to say there's one major thing that I did differently, it's to step outside of the school and to step outside of my parents for ways that I could think. Probably the best thing that I ever did was start acquiring business books at a fairly early age and reading them and implementing the information in those books.

Nicola : That's fascinating. You were always looking for ... you must have always, deep down, had a desire to run your own business, even when you were, well, when you did the lawnmower round, you did own your own business. I find fascinating as well the fact that you analyzed subconsciously, or consciously, that there were different types of customers, and that you'd rather go for the customers who've got the money to pay you to do less work, than the people who've got a bigger need but haven't got the money, perhaps.

James: Yeah. It's really an awareness that not everyone is the same and not every situation is the same. That within any set environment, there will be winners and losers. It's kind of like that Pareto principle that everyone's talking about, the 80/20 rule. I'm constantly applying that, but more so in a focused perspective. I take the top 20% of the top 20%. I'm looking for that 4% that delivers 64% of the results.

The real takeaway from that is, and I see it with students a lot, people are trying to do way too much. They're trying to cover far too much ground and it's consuming all of their time and attention. In much the same way people invest. They will take out a mortgage that uses up their entire disposable income, and there's nothing left for anything else. It's probably not the most effective way for them to move forward. Being aware of what you don't have to do is very important.

I didn't want to spend too long with the wrong type of customer, because I'd be ending up doing a lot more work for a lot less money, which means that my effective hourly rate was significantly lower, meaning that my time wasn't very leveraged. If I didn't feel that motivated about it I wouldn't do a good job, and it's not going to lead to referrals and I'm not going to want to get out of bed in the morning. By the end of it, I was able to do my entire lawn mowing round in one day by batching my jobs together and making sure that they were all geographically next to each other. There's a lot of lessons in that.

Nicola : Absolutely, and a lot of awareness on your part, so young.

James: I think so. I think awareness is something that is not common in society, whether you call it awareness or acuity, tuning in and observing what's happening and paying attention to things is the main skill that I learned by stepping outside the school system and outside the parent system because unfortunately, most people are just drifting through life in some kind of trance, and they're very blinkered by the way that they're conditioned as children.

Whether that's occurred in a country where they have a very fundamentalist beliefs and they get thrust a machine gin at age 10. Whether it's just the rich kid in Sydney heading off to private school in their little straw hat and suit, being taught The Church of England truths. We grow as a subject of our environment, and it's important to really have a good look at your environment and think, "Is this the right environment to get the results that I would like to have?"

Nicola : That's great. Really really interesting stuff. I grew up in an environment where there wasn't a lot of awareness, and there wasn't a lot of ... my mom was buying and selling properties, but she was mentally ill. She didn't really have the strongest grasp on reality. I've spent the rest of my life trying to catch up with that. I knew there was something missing, or I didn't know something, and I've spent the rest of my life looking for that and trying to learn it. You do have a sense somewhere that it's you in the end. Once you've learned all the tactics, then it's down, like you say, it's down to you, your behaviors and everything. But we're getting into the mind stuff too quickly. Let's go back to the lawn mower round and find out how you went from there to being such a successful car salesperson.

James: That was really a part time job and it ended abruptly. Big lesson from that. The short story is I went from my debt collection job, I was very good at that as it turned out, because of all the training I had from my grandfather as a timber broker. I was very good on the telephone, convincing people to pay their bills. I learned about making agreements and arrangements and a lot of the psychology that goes on with people who are in debt. I went from that through to credit, and from credit through to technology, and from technology, I was in a pretty role, I had a good pay. I was working for a trendy company at the time, back in 1995.

Nicola : Just after the dot com boom.

James: Vodafone. There's no real dot com boom in Australia. But digital telephony was big in 1993 and 94 and 95. It was really taking off and Vodafone was this cool, groovy company from the UK setting up. I was on about $35,000 a year salary and found out that I was about to have a baby in the family. It was like, "Well, hang on. My wife and I are both making $35,000 each, that's $70,000 for 2 of us, and we're about to have 3 people on $35,000. It doesn't work out. I'm going to have to get a job in sales, because I know that's where I can increase my income."

I walked across the road. I applied for a job at Toyota. They rejected me. They hired some mature lady from a clothing wear store. Then I went down the road to my next application which was the BMW dealership. I convinced this guy to give me a job. It was quite hard to get a job at this time, but he took a risk on me and within 12 months, I was the number BMW salesperson in the whole country.

The next year came around and they ripped me off a little bit with one of the recognition programs. They defrauded the points system, is the polite way to put it, and I felt miffed about that, so I switched brands to Mercedes Benz, where they welcomed me with both arms, and within a year of there, I was number one salesperson for Mercedes Benz. I realized now that it's not just luck, it wasn't just the area, it wasn't the product, there's something going on with the way that I'm doing this compared to my peers.

Being good in selling, I was at some point promoted into the role of manager, and from there I built my way up to general sales manager and from there I went to general manager. It was the last role that I held, but I worked in three different Mercedes dealerships through that transition period. I kept getting placed by Mercedes in new dealerships to go out and fix things up when they were broken. I was like a turn around guy.

Nicola : You weren't just good at selling, you were good at managing sales people, 2 usually mutually opposing roles, and it wasn't about the product, it was something in you was doing something different. Did you know? Were you able to analyze at the time what you were doing differently?

James: Yeah, of course. One thing that I had a great ability with was, aside from the selling side of it, was the paperwork side of it, and administration. Because I had come from administration and I'd studied in accounting, I could actually do paperwork and sell, which is pretty rare. That helped me a lot with management. I got really good at spreadsheets and stock sheets, and working out ratios and understanding what's happening with the business. That was definitely a skill set that helped me progress to the tole of general manager.

Also, I was a really good communicator by now because I'd spoken to thousands of people, face to face. It's a very, very competitive and stressful industry, the high level luxury automotive, it's a 100 year old industry, there's no room for error. It's always a monthly target. There's a lot of pressure and I really thrived in that environment because I was able to get better results than the other people doing the role. That lead to promotions and income increases and accolades and awards and a good reputation in the industry.

It was very good from that point of view and the income was good, but I really did sense that the majority of my customers, by observing them, I noticed they weren't employees for the most part, they were business owners. I figured that that's probably what I should be aiming to do next.

Nicola : How did you actually go about that?

James: I asked the owner of the business if he'd consider giving me equity. It wasn't off the table, but it was never forthcoming. One of my clients offered me equity in his business. I did all the due diligence and I formed a business entity and spoke to lawyers and accountants and I got a nice, big bill, nearly $10,000, to find out that this guy who offered me half his business was into other businesses that were cross collateralized with his business that he was offering a half share for me. It was very possible that if I went into that entity, I could have been sucked down the hole by his other entity. I couldn't take that move, but it really sped things up for me.

I was now getting very itchy to have my own business. At the same time I was learning about this Internet stuff, and I figured that I should learn how to build a website because I'd watch my parents new business, the travel agency, get sucked under by Internet people buying stuff online. Now it was really starting to take off in Australia, and we're talking about 2005. It's like 10 after the internet, Australia's sort of getting the hang of it. I figured this is something I need to learn how to do. I would set up my laptop at home and I would try and build a website and struggle with it terribly.

Nicola : It was html hard coding in those days.

James: I was trying all sorts of things. I tried Dreamweaver, and I tried this website builder that made things easy but it didn't work for search engines. I ended up buying some software that helped me build the site. I was so impressed with it, I built a test site with it to learn how it all worked. I put my affiliate link, and lo and behold, somebody actually bought the software from my site. It was $49.25.

Then I thought, I'm going to apply myself to this. I started putting some sales and marketing ideas to it. I created a bonus to complement the product. I started competing with other people in the market, I started running some Ad Words. I started blog posting and forum posting. I was able to jump that up to 2, and then 3, and then 5 sales. Then 10.

I sort of got a sense that I could probably put a lot more focus on this and really this could be something I could do instead of my job at some point. I created my first information product. Sold it. I made a $1000 a day when I sold my first information product for the first week. I thought, "Whoa, that's pretty much my salary, right there.

If I could just do this often, then this could be it." It took me a couple of years, about 2 and a half years, until I built up my business to the point where I was making the same as my salary. Then I stepped off into my own business. Basically, it was the transition from employee to business owner was one of a cross over period where I got very little sleep in the meantime.

Nicola :Also, you had kids as well. Trying to fit it all in must have been a bit of a challenge. What drove you on?

James: It was very challenging, and I'm quite stubborn. The fact that I was a high achiever in the corporate role, and it really pissed me off that it was so difficult online. Online is very difficult, and I would keep justifying my persistence with this idea that, "I'm not super stupid. I've got to be able to work this out." It took a long time and it was very frustrating, but I had a sense that it was possible because I had seen other people do it.

Eventually I got on an airplane and I went to America, I attended a conference. I sat side by side with other people and I won a prize that entitled me to go to a high level mastermind, and that high level mastermind, I was rubbing shoulders with people who were very successful at the time, like Mike Filsaime and Yank Silver and the guys from Stompernet which was big at the time. Seeing them making big sales soon made me feel that it's just a matter of time. People like Mike Filsaime were very encouraging and said, "You'll be doing 100 grand a month in no time." Which was good. I thought, "If he thinks I can do it and I think I can do it, I'm just going to keep doing this." 6 weeks later is when I quit my job.

Nicola : That's amazing and perfectly timed as well because we can now move into the business mind and talk more about that.

Mike saw something in you. Obviously all of your other employers have seen something in you. You knew it was in you to do it. What made the difference for you, psychologically speaking, what have you learned along the way that other entrepreneurs haven't yet learned that you'd like to share? You also interview so many amazing people on your podcast, what are your insights into what it takes, psychologically, to succeed online?

James: It's all about you and your mindset. There's no doubt about that. You have to do it yourself. One of the big things I see people do is they wish that someone else will do everything for them. This is what I call the lottery mentality. Those people that line up for the big lottery day buying their ticket. They're kidding themselves. They have more chance of getting run over on the way to the lottery ticket sales office than winning the lottery.

They've deferred responsibility to someone else. The first thing is, you have to be ultimately responsible for everything you have in your life right now and decide that you are committed to doing something about it in the future. First recommendation there is just get a mirror, look into it, the person you see staring back at you is the person who's going to take you to the next stage.

Don't think it's going to be someone else. You're not going to get it just paying big money for a program like a lot of these dreamers do. You're not going to get it because someone will gift it to you, it's only going to come from you. This self responsibility is a huge one and it's really lacking in business cycles. That's why a lot of employees are employees because they don't want to be responsible. They'd rather just have a guaranteed profit, and then go home and have a TV dinner and watch the latest soap opera than to step up to the plate. It does require a bit of fortitude.

You need to believe that if someone else can do it then you might be able to do it too. I think for the most part that is possible. If you can find anyone who's not quite as motivated as you or not quite as bright as you who's doing better than you financially or in a way that you'd like to be doing better, then take that as inspiration that it's possible.

Nicola : It's very true, because I've always had that sense inside that I was going to do something with business. That's never gone away. In spite of the ups and downs, I've always had that inner determination. I was on a mentoring call last night and somebody came on the line and said, "I haven't really done much this week, it's been Diwali." I thought, "That's fair enough. It's a big deal in your culture, but really you haven't even had time to put one thing every day on your Facebook page?" I just came off the call thinking, "Just not committed." People are just not committed to it.

James: That's exactly ... people don't have responsibility to themselves. They're happy to lie to themselves. The more honest you can be to yourself the better. That's one thing. The second thing would really be to think about what you're doing. What is it that you want? What are the steps to get it? Then commit to it. Just get doing it. It's not going to happen by itself.

Nicola : There's so many different things you can do to make money online. You have to decide which one is right for you. Then you have to have a deeper belief that the thing you pick is the right thing because you've chosen it and you're going to work it.

James: I tried a few different things, and I'm very pragmatic, so I work with the winners and I kill the losers. For me it was the software affiliate program that got my first $100,000. I worked with that. My business today, it doesn't have, it hasn't gone that far away from what always worked for me. I was really good with this software and I made information products and people purchased it.

Now, we build websites for people, we recommend software, like Lead Pages, and I help people grow their business with coaching. It's still pretty much the same need or problem being solved but in slightly different ways and much more leveraged because I've been able to scale it up with things like having a team and well trafficked and converting website. The core thing that worked for me, I just kept doing.

I think people put way too much blind faith out there. This just believing something, I'm sure there are a whole bunch of people who love the secret and all that, but I think it's mostly a load of crap. Just believing something isn't going to make it happen. You could believe in the tooth fairy all you want, it's not going to make the tooth fairy real. What you need to do is you need to start implementing the best guess that you can come up with and see what happens. If it doesn't work, don't be afraid to call your losses. One of the worst bits of advice I've ever heard about getting started online is, "Never give up." If your heading away from the watering hole in the desert, you want to stop real quick and turn around and head back towards the watering hole, because otherwise, you're going to die in the desert.

A lot of people are doing the wrong things without any validation, without paying attention, in this blind faith that it'll work. You don't have to blind online. The money leaves clues. It's easy to see where the money is. It's obvious that people selling stuff like Lead Pages are making affiliate commissions. You said it before, it's something people want and need, and don't want to give up. It does a great job and it's ethical. That's a good starting point. You don't have to guess. You know.

Nicola : If you were to go into the affiliate business, a recurring income, a recurring payment is one of the best ways to do it. If anyone wants to have a look at how James does it, or is doing it, go and have a look at superfastbusiness.com. I was really impressed with how simple the site is, how little distractions there are, how you lead people through to your, Own the Race Course, free training, then you've got daily video tips and your business building course, is that the coaching course?

James: Yeah, the whole community's actually on that site as well, there's simply a log in button on the top right for members, and there's a join button for people who aren't. Again, it's following the conventions, we expect that to on the top right of the side. That website is really a multi million dollar website, and it is simple. It has to be, otherwise a confused mind makes no choice.

Nicola : You've got a really interesting business model, haven't you, James? I think there's a recurring payment, but you put absolutely everything inside that membership, is that right?

James: Yeah, I've decided to package things differently to a lot of information marketers. I think most people do it wrong, of course, and I do it right. I teach my higher level students how to do it the way that I do it, and without exception, they've all made more profit with less effort, and that is to take the three main things that people want and put it into one place and to have a subscription. That is content, of course, the actual information, the community that's bringing other people together, because doing it alone is very hard online. If you go and buy one information product and download it onto your computer in isolation, I'm pretty sure you're probably not going to watch the whole thing, and you probably won't implement it. If you don't do anything, no one's going to call you on it. However, if you're in a community and people are talking about how excited they are and what they've implemented, you can see by the contrast in the same way that I did, that people are making good money not working for someone else, that it's possible. You might get inspired by that and you can share and you can be accountable.

The third thing is the coaching. That's where you have access to experts who are able to give you tips and pointers, instead of now just being a blind information product, you've got an active situation where you can have responses. You can ask a question is you're stuck. You can get further information. This whole community is, hopefully, one of those things that people won't want to give up because it adds so much value compared to what it costs.

Nicola : Yeah, that's a great point. I love the fact that you've got, presumably, not you anymore, experts in there, because people just get so hung up on making tiny decisions about their business. They really want to have someone to ask, "Is this right?"

James: The thing is, I think one of things that makes my community different to just about everyone else's is that I log into it every day and I have for 6 years. If I had a slogan on my business it would be that care more than any other expert. I really do care about the members, and I log in every single day to make sure that I'm adding value for members. But you're right, there's a lot of other experts. There's expert copywriters and eCommerce people and pay per click. Every type of strategy and every type of tactic, there are people in there who do it for a living. It's way way cheaper for a member to join a community like mine and ask any question on any topic and get an answer the same day than to have to go and pay for individual experts one on one.

Nicola : That's great. I remember my sister pointing out your business model to me a couple of years ago saying, "Look, look how James is doing it. That's so simple, but it's so powerful." Brilliant. You're still in there doing ... you never tire of it, do you? Never tire of helping people. People wonder why experts do it. It's because of the amazing feeling it gives you when somebody actually takes something that you've taught them and actually goes and does something with it.

James: One of the things is I only do things I want to do now, for the most part. It's an important part of the decision making process on what you should be spending your time and effort on. If you can choose between stuff you want to do versus stuff that you have to do, I'll put a line through the stuff that I have to do or that someone else can do and I'll have someone else in my team do that. I only do the things I want to do which means that when I do them I'm having a higher impact and it definitely flows through.

Nicola : Do you have a real office with a real team in it, or are they all virtual?

James: Everyone works from home, and I'm the only one in Australia.

Nicola : Right, so they're all around the world as well, fantastic. You really are walking the talk, as it were. Tell me about your business marketing. What really worked for you? How did you get the traffic flowing initially and what's working now?

James: My main philosophy, which I call, "Own the race course," is to have a website that you own where you put your good content. I like WordPress self hosted website, I like it on a nice fast server, and I on a demand that I control. I'm not going to build my business out on Facebook or YouTube or Linkedin or Pinterest or Google Plus, it's a huge mistake. I put good content there, and good content will be stuff that answers questions, that solves problems, that moves people to a better place than where they're at now that they can recognize. I will put it into multiple media formats, so they'll be video, they'll be audio, they'll be text, and they'll be images, and a mixture of some of those, all of those. I'll do it reasonably often because it's fairly easy to generate content when you're set up for it. That builds a long term asset of thousands of pages and posts over time, so it's constantly getting traffic. I get about 1000 downloads a day for my podcasts.

Basically, build your body of work, and then when you do post new stuff, you just let people know about it by sending them an email and share it on the social media platforms. That's when you do use those platforms to bring people back to your website. I call this the octopus method. You put all your good content at the head of the octopus, and then you share it down each of the tentacles. Send out your email. Tell your Google Plus, tell your Twitter, Facebook, Linkedin, just to places wherever your customers are at. Just let them know, "Hey, just posted this fantastic information graphic, or I just made a video about how to insert, solve a problem that they're probably experiencing right now.

Nicola : That's really key. It's interesting that you grew up in the early days of the internet because it was always about having your own website on your own server. As social media grew, people started building businesses on those platforms, which I've never really understood because logical thinking tells you you don't own those platforms. Like your lawn mower round, they can be taken away at any time.

James: I think that was a very valuable lesson for me.

Nicola : It was, looking back on it, you're thankful to that developer. Good stuff. What else? Tell me about the podcast, obviously as a fairly new podcaster myself, inspired by John Lee Dumas initially, hearing about his income really got my finger out and got me going again, but tell me about how your podcast got going and why you keep doing and how it started in the early days.

James: I used to do audio interviews before I podcasted. I've always done that because I've figured that's a rich medium and I was learning from mp3s as well. I wanted to do it and I did, probably 5 or 6 years ago. Then about 3 or 4 years ago, a friend of mine had me on his podcast show. I didn't really know much about it. It was a very popular episode, it was the most popular episode, and we made a stack of sales from it. It definitely got my attention. Then he invited me to co host a podcast with him. We set up a podcast called Freedom Ocean. I learned all about podcasts then. I learned about the plug ins and the set up and submitting to iTunes and all this stuff maybe 4 years ago at this time. From then, I went and added my regular blog as a podcast, I retro podcast all the interviews I'd already done, because you can back to it. You submit it and it fades it all up. I just kept doing it. I interview people like Clay Collins, etc. I've been doing this for 6 years of interviewing people.

Then I added a few more podcasts because the format works great. You're in this, everyone has an iPhone or Apple TV these days or an iPad. It's a great place to be. I set up other co hosted shows I have think [inaudible 00:40:06] with Ezra Firestone, I have Sales Marketing Profit with [inaudible 00:40:11] and I have Kicking Back with Joel Osborne. Then I've got my Super Fast Business Podcast where we put the audio version of any video we poured or just a dedicated interview. I ended up having multiple podcasts. They all bring subscribers and listeners. It's a great place to advertise your own products and services, which is my primary thing, then occasionally I'll have affiliated stuff. I'm not a fan of selling my space to someone else, I don't like the sponsorship model. I think that's not as good for the listener. If you compare free to ad TV to paid for movies, everyone wants the ad free version, so I much prefer that as a consumer and as a publisher.

Then of course I make sure that my products and services are really valuable, that they're recurring. For that reason, my effective rate and my profitability is substantially higher than pretty much all the other marketers than I'm looking at.

Nicola :I love the fact that you can just keep adding more stuff into your training course, the business building course, because you're constantly adding more value then and it just gets more and more value for money, and it becomes more and more of a great deal for people.

James: This requires a bit of a change in thinking. I want to tell you a big secret about subscription memberships, that it's actually not about the stuff. If I could have less stuff in there and someone could get a better result, that would be better for them and for me. It takes a more mature mindset to understand that it's not about stuff. Most people are stuck in the stuff mindset. Once you go beyond that, what you're really looking for is, how do I get the biggest result from doing the absolute least. Let's say an example, if you invest $10,000 in May and I'm a share trader, and then next month your portfolio's worth $15,000, and the next month it's worth $20,000, that's a better return on your time than having to consume 100 eBooks. You didn't have to do anything. You just had to put money there and then get a return.

My aim with members is to have them do the least things possible. I want to give them less stuff. I want to give them better questions. I want to have them thinking more. I want them to be doing the right things, and a lot less of them, than doing all the wrong things that everyone else does. When someone joins my membership, the goal is to get them to focus on one thing that they're going to do that will improve their business, and only that one thing. When they've done that, then they can move onto the next one thing.

Nicola : That involves your personal input, that's where the coaching comes in. Because people would join for the stuff, and then they would stay for the advice and the community.

James: Yeah, some of the things in there are trainings that will help them. For example, I've got a product in there called Inbox Relief. The whole purpose of that is to help people get rid of all the emails from their inbox. I show them the system that I use and how I stay with a clean inbox. Once they learn this and apply it, it's going to set them up much better than the typical scenario of having thousands of emails which are predominately marketing messages that are taking them away from the possibility of making any money at all because they're just victims of a marketing cycle that they haven't been able to get out because they made very poor choices. They signed up for all these marketers. They don't unsubscribe because they're weak, because they don't want to miss out on what the person's doing. They want to observe ... I can tell you what they're doing. They're selling to you, so now, unsubscribe.

That's why, as a marketer, the genius of having your Own the Race Course set up syndicate to all the different places where people are means that it doesn't matter if they're subscribed to you via email or not, necessarily, because you can still reach them on Facebook, you can still re market them with advertisements, you can still get them on YouTube or Twitter, because that's where most people are spending their entire day. They're basically sitting on Facebook for 8 hours with a clogged up inbox of 8000 emails. They got no traction. They're not getting anything done at all. That's the most common scenario.

Nicola :It's very true. Very true. I see it all the time. I love that. I love the single focus, the single minded focus you've got there, that's great. Before I learned to clear my inbox, I had 68,000 emails that were unread. I don't subscribe for many things and I unsubscribe from things, but once your email gets out there, it somehow gets passed around, I've got no idea how that happens. I've got, enroll.me, where it tells you how many new subscriptions you're on today and yesterday was 120 new subscriptions. I know I didn't sign up for 120 new newsletters. All the tools can help. Like you say, it gives you absolute clarity and doesn't distract you from the one thing you should be doing today to move things forward.

James: Well some of the very common ones, people subscribe to Facebook notifications. Is it really that important that you find out that you were mentioned in a post today or that you were tagged in a picture? Or can you just wait until you log in to Facebook next? Because that's probably going to be 20 minutes time. You don't need to subscribe to notifications. If you really want a quick fix, it's to go into your inbox and search for the word unsubscribe, and that will bring up all the newsletter emails. Just go an unsubscribe from as many as you can possible bear to unsubscribe from. Knowing that at any time you could rejoin that list in a heartbeat.

Nicola : Yeah, if you can remember who the person is. There's probably about 10 people that I love to hear from, I will open their stuff straightaway, but the rest of it just gets ignored until I'm ready. Wait else, is there anything apart from the podcast and the organic traffic? What else has worked for you in your marketing of your business? What one thing?

James: I think your email list is the most important thing to have.

Nicola : Totally agree. I've been building mine since 1998.

James: You were online 7 years before me, then.

Nicola : I'm a lot older than you, James! I accidentally stumbled across one shopping cart very early on in the process, and that's how I built my list because it had a little link at the bottom. You could actually put a little link at the bottom to say, "Forward this to a friend." Then the friend was able to subscribe straight from the email, which was an amazing thing.

James: I think your email list is very important, still the most powerful way to make sales is to set up a nice offer and to let people know about it at the right time and make sure it's good value for them and you will make sales. One of the things I do every year is I run a live event, it's once a year now. I can generate the 6 figures in sales just off a couple of emails just from when the tickets go on sale and that's the sort of power that's in the list when you look after it and you don't abuse it.

Nicola : Do you have a long series of follow up emails in the Andre [Chaperone 00:47:47] model or do you just have 7 and then people either buy or don't buy and then you just broadcast from there?

James: Firstly, I should say, Andre's a very good friend of mine, I speak to him every week.

Nicola : He's great, I loved his training.

James: Secondly, no. I don't have any, there's not 7, there's none lined up. I prefer to send fresh broadcasts for my primary newsletter. When someone gets and email from me, it's going to be I either just made it and sent it, or it'll be one of my automations, say they bought something, and I'm sending them their access, or they've visited a check out page and for some reason haven't purchased, I might just remind them that they were there and ask them if they're still interested. It might be an automated trigger. I use triggers, I use abandonment sequences, I use follow ups to purchases and feedback requests, but for my newsletter, it's all organic.

Nicola : So it's all coming from you in the moment?

James: Yes, because if you're going to make a coffee, you've rather have a fresh, barista made coffee than some instant coffee that was packaged and freeze dried 5 years ago.

Nicola : Again, you're doing things very differently to most people.

James: I hope so.

Nicola : That's great. Great advice for everyone. Tell me about your business money, James. You sound like you've always had an awareness of money, mainly from your grandparents and your parents. Then obviously your parents going through that experience where they lost their money must have woken you up even further. Have you always been good with money and managing it? Well, you've always been good with making it, obviously.

James: Yeah, I have been fairly interested in that. My parents having difficulty taught me about mortgages and loans and car leases. Debt collection taught me a lot about mismanagement of money. People have a tendency to buy things they can't afford. Especially even culturally. Whole countries have a completely strange mindset about living beyond your means. There's things that fuel that. I think in the

United States, for example, the government gives you a tax deduction for your own home mortgage, meaning people borrow more because of the tax deduction. You should never borrow because of a tax deduction. You borrow because you have to borrow and the tax deduction's like a bonus.

Where I'm at now is I have no debt. I've been debt free for 5 years. I don't like borrowing money for anything. I like to have cash reserves sitting in a bank account. It makes me feel more comfortable, which means that, it's one of the most important things possible, and it's something that, when I talk about it, you might resonate with, it removes desperation. There's nothing more cheesy and janky than a desperate marketer who needs money because they start to forget about the customer, and they're thinking only about themselves, and you can smell it and feel it, and it's just sleazy. If you can be debt free, if you can be in a position where you don't have any compromise financially, then it allows you to operate more in an organic and impactful way, I think. It comes through in everything that you do. You're never desperate, lazy, you're just doing things because it's the right thing to do.

Nicola : Yeah, makes decision making a whole lot easier, that's for sure. One of the things I learned from going bust is how little you can actually live on and so I determined, when I was in that place that when I started, when, not if, because I knew I was going to start making real money again, I would never load myself up with debt again because it was just crippling.

James: There's some interesting ideas from books like the 4 hour work week, for example, however, they kind of really only apply to young guys with no kids. It's not a very realistic thing. If you consider, I was a family guy of 4 kids, the average house price in Sydney is $850,000 as of last week, something like that. Tax rates are pretty much 50%. You'd need to make a lot of money to live as a family in Sydney. The best way to solve this is to make a lot more money. If you want to make a lot of money, you just create a lot of value and get it in front of as many people as possible. That's really the core of it.

Nicola : That's great advice. Do you invest in anything else, apart from your business?

James: Nope. I have cash reserves in a couple of different currencies, and I have my business. I don't really need much else. I own my car, I own my surfboards and my furniture. I'm happy not to be a share trader. I do currency trades because I take in a lot of income in different currencies, and I have to convert say, a US dollar to Australian dollar conversion. That can fluctuate quite a lot. I time it right. I make money when it's one to one, and then I'll sell it when it drops to 85 to 1.

It can be very beneficial to get the timing right. Then there's lots of fine tuning, things that I learned as a general manager. Here's a really simple one that almost nobody does, and that is as soon as you have a reasonable level of income, go to your fund provider, whether it's Pay Pal or a credit merchant facility, and ask them for a better rate. In my case, I was able to go from 2.7 to 1.1 for Pay Pal. On a few million dollars a year, one and a half percent makes a big difference.

Nicola : If you do the math, that is really quite astonishing, isn't it? People just, I went, on this weekend with Rich Chevron a couple of weekends ago, and he sent us out on a quest. The quest was all about just asking people for things and for help. So many of the people in the room had such a big issue with that, and that is what it's about. It's about having the balls to ask.

James: Yeah.

Nicola : Which you've obviously got in spades. Good stuff. Thank you very much. I really really enjoyed talking to you. Tell us what you're looking forward to over the next year, what's Super Fast Business and James Schramko got in store in the next year?

James: It's really simple for me. I just want to be a significantly better surfer by this time next year, that's my primary goal at this point.

Nicola : That's a very worthy goal.

James: It is because it means that my business continues to run on the right schedule and that I'm able to do that every single day and develop that. So much of the thinking time and the metaphor for the challenge or improvement is transferable across. Even though your not near a keyboard or an internet connection, it doesn't mean your brain turns off. It's really a very soulful and worthwhile pursuit. It was the sport of kings, so I think it's good enough for me.

Nicola : If people want to come to your event next time, they need to come over to superfastbusiness.com and get on your mailing list, because that's how you promote it by the sounds of it, and they can check out your Own the Race Course training and video tips. I'd just like to thank you very much for spending an hour with me, James. I really appreciate it.

James: Thanks for having me. Hopefully there's been some interesting topics that make people think. Some of it might cause resistance. Some people might dislike some of the things I've said, but it's really point is I want you to think differently than the way everyone's talking about it, because there is a different. Certainly, on my site, the live event is just /live. We've got a page talking about it.

Nicola : That's brilliant. I'm going to get myself to Australia at some point and get over there. Thank you very much and have a great evening.

James: Thank you so much.

Visit James at SuperFastBusiness.com

2. JENI HOTT

Nicola : Today, I'm joined by Jeni Hott who is considered to be the highest earning blogger in the world. In fact, she's one of the few seven figure bloggers in the industry. She pursues what she calls her extreme passive income strategies, which have allowed Jeni to travel the globe for four years while working only a few times a year, and still earning millions of dollars. Recognized by Google as one of the most widely read bloggers on the web with over 100 million visits and growing, Jeni collaborates with both Google America and Google Latin America for testing and general insights on AdSense.

Jeni has recently accepted a request to create a blogging course for universities across the US that will also be available for veterans uncovered by the GI Bill. She's a featured entrepreneur in Living Dot Com documentary released summer 2014, which we can highly recommend because we saw it early last weekend. She's just become Jeni Hott, as she's recently married to rock musician Steve Hott. Welcome to the call, Jeni, I really appreciate you joining me today.

Jeni: Thank you. It's such a pleasure.

Nicola: The funny thing was that I heard of you, and I've been telling this story on the podcast for a while. First, while sitting on a sun lounger in Grand Turk with your friend Margaret and her son Tyler.

Jeni: That's right, I heard about that. Such a small world, isn't it?

Nicola: Especially when you take the virtual world into account as well. Tell us about Jeni Hott. Where did you grow up, what kind of background do you come from, how did you become an entrepreneur?

Jeni: I come from a long line of entrepreneurs. That was something that was instinctive in me. I didn't really like working for other people or for other corporations. I grew up in California, but I went to school on the east coast at Rutgers. I ended up working in the corporate world doing PR, and I just despised it. It was just horrible. You know how the corporate world is. Just not the most liberating industry to be in.

Nicola: I've never lasted more than 18 months in a proper grownup job.

Jeni: See that? We're not suitable to be employed by others. I ended up working in the typical corporate world where I was in it to achieve a goal. I was working for a boss I just could not stand. She was just a nightmare. She's not a nice person. I saw so many of my friends getting laid off and fired. The politics there was just horrible. So, I just decided to make a change. One day, I just realized, "I've got to do something because this isn't what I want to do. This isn't where I see myself for the rest of my life." One day, I just decided to give my things away, packed up, and moved to Puerto Vallarta, Mexico.

Nicola: Where did you move from? Where had you been living up until that point?

Jeni: I was back and forth between New Jersey, from Princeton, to New York.

Nicola: Then you went down to, is it New Mexico, did you say?

Jeni: No, Mexico. The actual Mexico. To Puerto Vallarta, which is actually paradise. But it was still quite a culture shock.

Nicola: Had you been there before?

Jeni: I had. I've gone down and visited with my grandmother just a typical vacation and I just fell in love with it. I just thought, wow, this is just such a cool, relaxed place, such a different atmosphere, different environment than New York. Also, too was I loved the qualities that people had there, the values. Such a different thing than I had ever experienced. Everybody was so happy but they had so little. It was just the total opposite of what I was used to. It really resonated with me and I just felt like I wanted to do something different, I wanted to make some changes and I wanted to make sure that I was on a path that I was going to be happy, not stuck in a corporate world. I already knew I was miserable.

Nicola: Now, I don't know if you've been warned, but I ask questions that other people don't ask. So, do tell me to be quiet if you don't want to answer any.

Jeni: I think that's wonderful.

Nicola: Did you happen to ...

Jeni: I am ...

Nicola: Did you have a big pot of cash when you went down there or did you live on your wits?

Jeni: No, not at all. Not at all. I had some saved up, but not much. For the following year I was taking on just freelance PR jobs and the following year I made about $13,000, for the year. I know, that's even less than pounds. No money whatsoever. I had this one particular client who was, to say she wasn't a nice person would be really putting it nicely, so I went to go visit her one day and this led to the most defining moment of my entire life.

I went to go visit her and standing in her shop, and she starts screaming at some people that tried to come into her shop before it was open.

Nicola: Oh nice.

Jeni: And I just thought, "wow, this is crazy." The way that she was speaking to me, the way that she was speaking to other people. I had gotten up early to be there for her and I was leaving and I thought, "wow, this isn't much different than what I was doing back in New

York." And I just thought, I don't know why I came here if I'm going to be doing the same thing.

I was walking back and there's this famous street in Puerto Vallarta and it's very old. It's nothing but cobblestones and these old lanterns and cute little lanterns and stuff. I stopped on these cobblestones and just had this moment where I just had this moment. One of those epiphany moments that just happen once in a lifetime. I looked down at my feet on these cobblestones and I started thinking. And I thought, "this isn't what I want. This isn't why I moved down here. This isn't what I was going for." I just decided to make some changes because I thought about all these things I don't want, and I thought, this is great. Now I know what I don't want so now I can decide what I really want and I can go for that.

So I stood in the street, on those cobblestones. People must have thought I was nuts because I stood there for another hour and just went on this rant in my head about all the things that I wanted in my life. I want to travel the world, I want to make endless amounts of money, I want to work on my own schedule, I want to be able to sleep in until noon if I want to. I want to be able to buy my parents a house if I want to. I just sent on this rant about all these things I wanted and when I was done, I stopped and I thought, all right, I'll make a promise to myself right in this moment. I will never again do anything that makes me sacrifice all these things that I want in my life. I did that. I've kept that promise to myself since that day. I went home that day ...

Nicola: I was going to say, what did you do next?

Jeni: I went home that day, I was in my condo, and I thought, "what can I do that will let me have this life I just decided I was going to have?" I thought, people are doing some stuff online, people are making some money there so why don't I take a look and see what will work for me? So, I started looking online and I found some people who were making a little bit of money. Making like $2 grand. I think

Joel Comm, at the time he's making about $500 a day. I thought if he can do it, I can do it.

Nicola: He was an Ad Sense expert wasn't he?

Jeni: Yes the Ad Sense Code. Real nice guy too. So, I started looking at what he was doing and I took a look at a few other bloggers. Blogging at the time was so primitive, you couldn't really do much with WordPress at the time, it was still so new. A few sites talked a little bit about making money online. Came across a few little tips and just started working. It took me testing things out, seeing what I wanted to do here and there. I decided to set my first goal as making $33 a day. So, today this is my favorite number, still. $33. So, I decided that I was going to make $33 a day because then my rent was covered, all my bills were covered. In Mexico, you can live comfortably on that. You could at the time. It took me a few months to hit that $33 a day. There is nobody to learn from then, it's all trial and error.

Nicola: I was going to say, how did you know what to do?

Jeni: It was just trial and error. A lot of mistakes, a lot of new discoveries. But it's cool because every time I hit a mistake, well, lost money today. It was great because I learned how to make a lot more the following day. It was really good thing. And the following month ...

Nicola: When are we talking about Jeni? Let me just place this in a timeline.

Jeni: This was 2005 or 2006.

Nicola: Okay.

Jeni: Around the end of the year there. So, my next month I made $66 a day and my next month I made $99 a day and it just kept going up. By the end of the first six months, I had worked so hard that my wrists were bruised. Just black, blue, purple, you name it, all the way up and down. I'm wrapping them in Ace bandages like crazy and taking Advil every few minutes and I worked until I literally couldn't lift my wrists anymore. If I picked up a glass of water I would be crying, I would have tears just coming down my face and I finally stopped and I went, all right, now I'm going to change all those things.

I'm going to decide a few things so that this never happens again. I promised myself then that I would never again work so hard that this happens. Never be this hard on my body. I made a promise that I would never again, because I asked myself again, what do I want? I realized that I want to be able to travel the world, I want to be able to stay three or four months somewhere if I want to. I want to at least stay for a month so I don't want to have to work for that much time if I'm going to be doing that. So, I made a promise to myself that I would never again implement any strategy that made me have to work than once every three or four months. [crosstalk 00:11:47]

Nicola: For the benefit of people listening, there's going to be a lot of people listening, thinking, "Well, I'm willing to work hard." What were you doing specifically? You were blogging, but what specifically were you blogging about and how were you making the money?

Jeni: My first site was a travel site. It was a travel site about Puerto Vallarta. It's interesting. I haven't thought about that in so long. It was a travel site about Puerto Vallarta and I was basically just writing content and then putting AdSense on it. I remember the first few days I would call my mom, so excited, "Oh my gosh, I made 99 cents today." 20 cents, 30 cents, 90 cents and every time it would go up I'd be like, "$2 today," and she would just be so excited. It took me a couple of months to hit that $33 a day, but then once I did it just kept going up. $33 to $66 to $99.

Nicola: You were blogging on such a tight topic. Every post you put up had long tail keywords in it and Google just loved that at the time.

Jeni: You know, I didn't really think much about the SEO side at all. In fact, to this day, my largest site has a lot of pages that still rank really well because they were never SEOd. It was still so fresh at that time. I think, there was only one really big name in SEO then, which was Brad Cowan. And I listened to a few of his things, but most of it I just focused on my readers, which I still do today.

Nicola: That's really interesting because a lot of people feel that they need to do a lot of sneaky SEO to get ranked by Google, but still, you do get rewarded if you have a site that is human-focused.

Jeni: Yeah, I think that, SEO, there's a few basic foundations that you want to do so that you can help the search engines understand what your site is about, what your page is about. There's a few basic things but focusing on SEO and putting all your effort, I think, is the kiss of death because if you think about the purpose of search engines, their goal is to provide the best possible results for their searchers. So, if you're focused on that too, you're only focused on those searchers those readers, then you're always going to be serving the best possible information for them. So, the search engines are naturally going to keep raising their standards, and, instead of having to meet their criteria for these, it's just the bigger picture is going to be, okay, this site really does provide the best information we're always going to serve them is #1.

Nicola: I've tried occasionally to write a blog post that's geared towards a certain word and it just kills your creativity and it doesn't flow at all, it just sounds so wooden.

Jeni: Exactly, and I think people and search engines can see through that. I think it's just better to focus on people. I think that, since we're moving now towards an age where it is totally social media popularity contest, I think that's a huge sign, huge evidence to me that we're moving towards meeting the readers' needs over the search engines because, in the end, you can't fool the search engines when it comes to popularity.

Nicola: So you've got your travel site up and it's getting pennies a day and you're building up to dollars a day. How many pages would you say you had on that site before you started making money?

Jeni: Probably about 100.

Nicola: Did you have to go out and do research or were you gathering all the information for that site about that particular place online or were you actually going out into the area and finding out things to write about?

Jeni: It was a lot of stuff, I always wrote about what I already knew. It was just easier that way. I didn't know then what I do now is to see what people are searching for and then, if I know about it, I provide information on that but at the time I just stuck to writing what I knew. So, a lot of it even was, I'm lucky that it happened to be what people were searching for.

Nicola: Because you were on the ground and you were going to the cool restaurants, and the clubs and bars and things, so you knew about it.

Jeni: Exactly. Exactly.

Nicola: That's great. So, what did you go on to after the travel site?

Jeni: A health site, which is now my largest site. This is the one that had over 100 million hits and growing. Actually, it was 100 million hits in January of 2013 so I don't even know what it's at now.

Nicola: If it's growing exponentially it doesn't even bear thinking about.

Jeni: Exactly.

Nicola: Did you have an interest in health yourself or did you just realize that there were a lot of people that had an interest in that.

Jeni: It started out as a niche site and it just got so big that I just started expanding to general health and eventually it became one of the most read health sites on the web. It's HDIHealth.com.

Nicola: Okay. So you're still doing all the work yourself at this stage? You're not outsourcing or anything?

Jeni: No. For the longest time, I figured out a few tricks. If you remember I said that I wasn't going to implement any strategies that made me have to work more than once every three or four months. So, I started to think. How can I automate this? How can I automate the content? How can I automate getting new content without actually having to write it myself? What I did, I started using traditional media. Press releases. Which I do now.

A friend of mine owns a company called PR Reach and I use them a lot. They send out press releases. That was the difference between hitting thousands of people coming to my site, sorry, tens of thousands, to millions. That just sent a huge spike. Once I did that, I thought, okay, how can I get more content but not have to actually write it myself?

What I did was implement forums and then I just started thinking again about the needs of humans ... I'm very big on this now. The six human needs. Maslow's Six Human Needs. Are you familiar with that? For those who don't know, in my hierarchy, number one is contribution. Always feeling the need to give and to provide to serve people. My number two is growth. I'm always wanting to learn the lesson from whatever, I want to learn more, I want to feed my mind. My number three is love and connection. That is usually the number one for everyone. For most people that is number one.

That's exactly why I put those forums in because it meets that need. The next one is uncertainty, I believe. For variety. We all have this need for variety for different things in our lives. The next one is significance. We all have the need to feel special in some way. Some people think it's a bad thing. It's not. It's totally normal. We all have that need and there's different ways you can feed that. My last one is certainty, which, thank goodness that's my last one. That means I have no problems booking flights last minute and not knowing where I am going to stay for that night or, I don't have to have a lot of certainty in my life which is a very, very good thing.

They say that the amount of certainty you have, that you rely on for happiness, the more unhappy you'll be. So, that's a good thing if that's something you can deal with. If I apply that ... what's that?

Nicola: I was going to say where, sorry there is a slight delay on the line, where did you find out about your core needs? Did you do a course or is there somewhere online you can go to find out what they are?

Jeni: I'm a huge, huge, huge, huge Tony Robbins person. Anthony Robbins? Which I know he comes to London quite a bit. I absolutely love him and I've learned all this from him. The majority of it.

Nicola: Yeah because I did a coaching course with Coach University in America, a distance learning course and that was back in 98-99 and I learned all about core needs and core values which were probably derived from Tony's teaching probably.

Jeni: Well it came from Maslow initially, but there are a lot of gurus that, I use that word loosely, but a lot of gurus that teach a lot of the self-development of using the psychology and the needs of humans.

Nicola: It helps, it really does, if you know what your core needs and your core values are and some of mine crossover. So, learning, you've got the same one. It's a core need for me and it's also one of my highest values. I enjoy it the most and it give me pleasure and joy but it's also one of the things I need to function.

Jeni: I love that. That's a really good one to have really high.

Nicola: It means you never get bored, that's for sure.

Jeni: That's exactly true.

Nicola: Okay, so, you've got your biggest site up now and you're traveling the world. Are you traveling the world yet or are you still living in Mexico?

Jeni: No, I didn't. And once I implemented the forums, again, I was starting to think about the six human needs and how can I meet this and all of my readers? Once I started thinking about the psychology of it, I realized that, they say that if you reach, what is it they say, if you reach three or more of the human needs for people in general than you have raving fans. Well, I try to meet them all. I always joke that I don't have raving fans, I have love slaves.

Once I got everything going really well and I started automating everything, I figured out different automation systems that would allow me to not have to work those three or four months. Sometimes I would go a little bit longer, I don't advise that, but, it became really easy to just automate everything. I would sit down and write something once every six months or so, write a few blog posts, and schedule them to go out. So, it became really simple. But once I did that it didn't take me too long to hit six figures. I had told myself that once I hit six figures a month, I would go on vacation. I would just start traveling the world for a year. I would do whatever I wanted, see whatever I wanted, spend whatever I wanted for a year. That year turned into, well, four years.

Nicola: I've got so many questions on that I don't know where to start. Let's go back to the forums for a minute. Forums are notoriously hard to get going.

Jeni: They are.

Nicola: You don't sound like you have any fear of things not working. You also, presumably, had to work quite hard to get the forums going, or did you just have so much traffic by then that when you launched your forums, people just started using them.

Jeni: Because I was using those press releases, I would get picked up on the news. I would get picked up on the 5 o'clock news, I would get picked up on the morning shows. Then my traffic was coming so fiercely that I had no problems starting those forums. But this was, I will say this, this was the second time I did try to start forums. The first time did not take. The second time it took really fast.

Nicola: That's really a momentum, critical mass kind of thing, is it?

Jeni: Absolutely. Absolutely.

Nicola: And when you say you're using the press releases you're taking the content from the press releases and putting them on your site as a blog post but presumably crediting the source as well.

Jeni: No, no, no. I would write press releases. At the time when I was starting out, I didn't really want to spend too much money on different things, I was testing things out. So, I'd write my own press release at the time through PR Web, which now ... it's not my favorite. I prefer PR Reach, but I would submit it there and it would just be picked up across the news. It would have my website and it would send traffic to my website.

Nicola: That is such a genius strategy. I can't believe it. So there's that trial and error thing again. You're just thinking all the time, what can I do that's going to bring me more traffic? How can I serve my readers better? And then you moved into how can I automate everything so I don't have to work so hard?

Jeni: Exactly.

Nicola: Wow. That's great. So tell me about your year off that turned into four then. Again, that's a really brave thing to do. Did you just book a flight somewhere? Or did you have friends where you were going?

Jeni: I did. I think I hit a few more places in Mexico first. I went to Cancun, I went to Cozumel, I went to Cabo. I went to, I think I went to Cayman Islands, which I absolutely loved. Loved the Cayman Islands. Went to a few places in Canada. Then I went to Fiji. Spent about a year back and forth from Australia and Sydney and Melbourne and Melvin. Went all over Australia. Went to London, Dubai, Israel. Oh man, I've been to so many places it would take me awhile, I'd probably forget a bunch. I just floated around and had a blast.

Nicola: Traveling on your own or did you have someone with you?

Jeni: No, I always seemed to have friends that are going somewhere. Like my friend just last year asked me, "do you want to go to Argentina?" She wanted to look at vineyards and we wanted to learn how to tango. So, we took off to Argentina for a month.

Nicola: That sounds like ...

Jeni: Actually, that was Margaret that you met.

Nicola: Yes, I did indeed. And learned so much from. I interviewed her just recently. She's, for anyone listening it's Margaret, her interview was actually fascinating because she's doing some amazing work with teen mom orphanages.

Jeni: Yes. In Peru. She's such a brilliant woman too. Just such a brilliant soul.

Nicola: Well, she took her teenage son, Tyler, on the cruise and everybody just loved him. He was so much fun. Good stuff. And you just meet some amazing people when you're just traveling around like that I suppose?

Jeni: Absolutely, absolutely.

Nicola: And you keep in touch with everyone because you can and the internet just makes that so much easier nowadays doesn't it?

Jeni: It really does. What would we do without the internet?

Nicola: I don't know. You were without it earlier and having a little panic.

Jeni: Yeah, that wasn't fun.

Nicola: Good stuff. Okay, so, I'm still turning over all this information and what I'm trying to distill out of it, your story, is what other people can take. I know we're going to talk about what you're looking forward to next year, I know that you've got some plans to help other people. I love the veteran and GI course, that just sounds really incredible because people who have been disabled can, hopefully, still use the internet. If I was going to ask you, what out of your story is most important for new entrepreneurs to know in terms of mindset, what would you want to share?

Jeni: I have this golden rule that has served me so well. It always takes awhile to get people to really adapt to it. It's not easy. Even when I'm starting something new, or when I'm guiding someone new. It's not always easy to stick to it, but once you do, everything becomes so easy. So, I tell everyone, focus on 80% adding value and 20% on the technical side. The money making, the SEO, don't worry about that stuff so much. If you focus the majority of your efforts and your energy on adding value and serving your readers you will be amazed at how fast and how easy the money comes and the people come. It's just extraordinary.

But, like I said, it does take some adapting. Even when you think you're doing it, you have to go back and question yourself because, "what's my intention here?" Because it is easy to get sucked into the money side and be like, "wait a minute", and I have to go back and say is this really serving my readers at the absolute peak? That's a tricky one but once you master that it's just bliss. It's just so easy.

Nicola: It must make you feel real good as well, it's not like selling. I remember when I first read Think and Grow Rich - Napoleon Hill, strange book in some ways, but there was a phrase in it that struck me and I've never forgotten ever since. It said something along the lines of, "if you can find the greatest number of people to serve then rivers of abundance will flow for you." I stood there in the middle of the room, and I can still remember the room I was in when I read that and

I just thought, "he means the internet," and it hadn't been invented then.

Jeni: Oh wow. I do remember that. I remember that in the book.

Nicola: Such a wonderful analogy. Work serving your readers and, even when you think you're serving them, ask yourself again, "am I really serving them?"

Jeni: Absolutely, absolutely. The other thing I would suggest to people is when you have setbacks, because I promise you your entire internet career you will have setbacks, there will be things that come up. The other day I just had over a million pages de-index from the internet, just immediately. Within like ... yes. But it happens and every time something like that happens, it's funny, is I actually kind of get happy because I know that I'm about to learn a lot and I know that I'm going to be helping more people and making more. Most people would think I am nuts when I'm like, "oh my god, well this sucks but this is so awesome."

Nicola: Gives you something to do I suppose.

Jeni: It kind of does. But I learn so much when something like that happens and that's what gets you to the next level. If you were just steadily making money and doing well you're not going to be going up, you're not going to be going anywhere, you're not going to be achieving the next level. You have to fail a little bit in order to get to that next step.

Nicola: One of your core values is to learn. So it's like rubbing your hands together and saying , "yes, loads more good stuff to learn."

Jeni: Yeah, yes. And I wouldn't say that you have to fail to get to that next step. I shouldn't put it that way. I should say that that's what gets you there the fastest. That'll get you there the fastest and most efficient way. It's just you're going to get there so quick when you make a little, hit a road bump.

Nicola: For the people listening, thinking, "I've got a family, I've got a job, I can't possibly sit and pound the keys until my wrists are sore like you did. What gave you that absolute determination because I watched your presentation at the speaker's summit, [inaudible 00:30:15] Summit, and you were telling that story and I remember thinking, you were saying how your friends were coming in to get you to go out and you just wouldn't go out, you were so fixed and determined on succeeding with this. Where did that come from inside you?

Jeni: I was so focused on that life that I wanted. It just was leverage. I just stayed focused. That's what I wanted and nothing was going to pull me away from it until I got there.

Nicola: A lot of people struggle with the belief that it's going to work for them, the belief that it'll work for anyone, let alone the belief that it will work for them. Did you have an absolute deep sense of belief that you were going to crack it?

Jeni: Yes. I knew without a doubt. In fact, my mom would say, she'd ask me what I was doing, my friends would ask me, "are you coming back to the States? What are you doing? This is crazy," but, I just knew. I just know. I know I'm going to do this. I'm not going anywhere until I do this, I just knew. I absolutely knew.

Nicola: I find that awesome. The complete focus, the complete determination, and the complete belief. If more people, more entrepreneurs, had those three things then they would just crack on and not let anyone distract them or get in their way would be amazing.

Jeni: Absolutely.

Nicola: Anything else you want to share for a new entrepreneur about your mindset? How do you keep yourself, in the early days, do you have any rituals that you would use to keep yourself focused and positive?

Jeni: I didn't really have any rituals or anything. I just stayed focused. It wasn't like I was trying to stay focused, I wasn't trying to do anything except, I was just going from A to Z. I was so focused on Z because I knew that's what I wanted. That's the life I wanted, that I was just so pointed in that direction I couldn't see anything else.

Nicola: Had you already been to Tony Robbins stuff by then or did you get into that later?

Jeni: No, I had gone to one ages before. Before I moved to Mexico. That was one of the things that set me on that path too was that I realized I'm not crazy. I can do whatever I want. If I don't want to do the corporate ladder thing, I don't have to. That was something huge. What was funny was that when I went to go back I wanted to, I had reached my six-figure mark and I was like, "all right, I want to go travel the world now. I want to go do what I promised myself I would do."

Well, I called to go back to another one of his entry-level events, which is UPW. I called and I talked to my families' rep, their representative and they said, "oh, he's not here anymore. Now he's the concierge for his platinum partnership." And I said, "I don't even know what that is." And she said, "it's this special thing they have set aside for people that want this one-on-one experience with Tony for a year. Only 100 people are allowed in a year, you have to apply, it costs this much money," I'm thinking that it was about $135,000 for the year, for the trips and everything.

I said, actually she didn't even tell me how much it was, but I just said, "you know what, I want that." And she said, "what, wait, I need to tell you what it would involve and everything, you'd need to talk to them, you need to do this." I said, "I've got to be somewhere in 15 minutes, here's my card. I'm going to go." To this day it's a joke with Tony and his brother-in-law that they think it's hysterical that I'm the first and only person who signed up over the phone without even knowing what it was. I was like, "I gotta go, but ..."

Nicola: But I want it.

Jeni: Yeah, exactly. And then, I think about a month later, I got an email saying your first trip is coming up and you're going to Fiji to Tony's resort there. I was like, in a month, all right. I've had another trip planned, or something planned and I moved that around. I had no idea what I was in for, but next thing I know I'm hanging out with Tony and getting one-on-one advice with him and it was amazing. The majority of my friends that I've traveled with, including Margaret, I know them from this program. From this platinum partnership with him. That's something that only this lifestyle and only this amount of freedom and this money that you're making from the internet, something like that, those experiences are exactly what I wanted so it was just such a blessing.

Nicola: That's amazing. I think the only thing that could possibly come close to that would be spending some time with Richard Branson on his island. That's one of the things that I would really like to do.

Jeni: Hey, if he comes up with a platinum partnership of his own I will be there. He's one of my heroes I would love to meet him.

Nicola: I get the distinct impression he's not, he doesn't like things that organized, he likes things a bit more laid back.

Jeni: Yeah, darnn it.

Nicola: Good stuff. What would you, you're just getting going on, I mean, was it the film coming up that made you start thinking, I need to do this, I've been skulking around your website so I know you've got some coaching programs coming up and everything, was it the film that was the catalyst for you to get all this stuff going?

Jeni: You know what, it was. When I said before that I wouldn't recommend people going more than three or four months without working, well I started to. I went a couple years where I was not working for like a year at a time and I got so detached and I lost my drive and I started to think, I don't feel like I have a mission anymore. The sites are still doing great, I'm still traveling. I think I was even in

Australia at the time but I want to do something big. The next thing I know I get this phone call from a producer in New York saying we're interviewing entrepreneurs and we've heard your story and we want to know if you'll be in this movie for us. I had to think about it. I didn't just jump on it right away.

But, when he was telling me that half of our jobs in the United States alone, I don't know the numbers for the UK, but when they told us that half of our jobs are going to be disappearing in the next twenty years and going to outsourcing and to the internet, I just thought about it and I thought, wow, I have friends who have been laid off repeatedly in the last year. I have so many friends who can't find jobs and things like that, from college, and I just realized, wow, I have so much knowledge now from what I've gone through and from what I've experienced that I feel this responsibility to share it.

So, it was such a huge thing for me to start learning about. The state of the economy and what's going on. Where our future is headed and to know that I could actually help with that, yes, that's what spurred me to go to the next, what I'm doing now.

Nicola: So the film is going to help you a lot with the marketing of your own business that you're forming now, and what other type of marketing will you be doing do you think? What would you recommend new entrepreneurs look at nowadays for marketing their businesses?

Jeni: Well, I'm launching a new site that actually will have training in all different areas of internet marketing and internet entrepreneurship that actually just teaches you how I do what I do, but not just myself, other gurus. So I have friends that are very well known authorities in SEO, authorities in social networking, you name it. We're all putting together our own coaching programs that will help people to learn how to do what we do. So, you can come to the site, it's called Brilliant, Etc - brilliantetc.com.

You can sign up now, it'll be launched in the next week or so. Basically, you can select whatever you want to learn. You have the opportunity to just get free trainings, or you can get some other ones that each individual authority will be able to provide their own training or their own personal view if they want to. But in addition to that, you'll also be able to interact with them because we'll have forums set up that once you're enrolled in their program, you'll actually be able to be informed and be in contact with those authorities so you can go right to the source to ask them to clarify things or ask their opinion on things, or get their feedback, which is completely invaluable.

Nicola: Yeah, and the other thing I found really interesting when I was looking at your site is the kind of people you've got involved in this project are not your average household, well household names, nobody is a household name in the internet, but they're not the names that you see all the time are they? They're not the big, well-known gurus. They're under-the-radar experts that you obviously know to be genuinely doing their thing.

Jeni: Yeah, you know what's funny, our household names, they're household names but in the internet marketing world. It's kind of funny. It's not mainstream by far but I think those people are coming. I think that's our future. I think the next celebrities, rock stars, I think those are going to be internet people. I'm really excited to see what comes in the next 20 years or so but, who knows, maybe it'll be somebody who learned it from Brilliant, Etc. I hope.

Nicola: That would be nice, wouldn't it?

Jeni: Yeah. Now is definitely the time.

Nicola: Yeah. I know that you went to the premiere of the film and I know it's been released online now because we bought it and downloaded it and watched it only last weekend. Do you know how the film is doing because that's got to be the biggest PR thing for you surely?

Jeni: It's doing amazing. The feedback has been extraordinary. I know that they are planning a lot more screenings. I do believe that they'll even be doing a screening in London. I know it will be passed around Russia. They are putting it in, I think, 12 different languages just to start. They're really on a mission to bring awareness to the shift in our economy.

Nicola: Yeah, and I think the fact that there are so many people on there who are quite obviously living the life they were talking about was a really good thing to help people believe that it's possible because so many people are cynical. I remember before I started personal development I wouldn't even buy decent make-up and hair stuff because I just didn't believe it worked. So, when you suspend your cynicism your life starts to improve somewhat, not to mention your hair. It's easy to be cynical, though, isn't it because that stops you from having to take any action.

Jeni: Absolutely, but you know what? If you think about it, what you have to lose is that whole future that you could have.

Nicola: That's really cool. Yeah, the opportunity cost of the future you could have had. Amazing. So, what about money, Jeni? You obviously have had money, you've got lots of money and then you've also had no money. How have you learned to manage a lot of money like that? Did you, are you a naturally careful person or did you have to take lessons, or did you have to get a coach? How did you go from having no money to managing lots of money well?

Jeni: You know what's very interesting is that there's been times when I've gotten hit by things. Especially living out of the country. It's expensive. It's expensive to do the exchange and it's expensive just to travel that much and everything, so, I took a few hits, but I always, same thing with how I learned internet entrepreneurship, every time I would get hit by something, I would come back stronger. I would learn more from it.

I'm really grateful now that my other half is actually, got me checking price tags on things. That was my New Year's resolution was to start checking price tags on things. Now's time to prepare for our future, so. It's the same thing. You learn as you go along.

What's interesting is I've, I was approached by a financial advisor years ago that explained to me how a lot of rock musicians and sports, what do you call them, athletes, professional athletes, how they come in to money so fast. They literally go from zero to having millions in the bank overnight and how they end up going through the same lessons and stuff.

It's interesting to learn from other people's experiences before you have to go through them. You never have to go broke because you know, this is a good thing to keep in mind that just because I'm going from zero and I want to spend like absolute madness the first couple years, you don't ever have to get to the point where some people have to declare bankruptcy and things like that. You just learn from other people's experiences too.

Nicola: Yeah. Do you invest in anything else? Do you invest in gold or real estate or jewelry or?

Jeni: You know, I haven't in the past. I was too busy having fun, but now I am. I'm getting ready to start playing with some real estate. Margaret is doing real estate coaching, my friend Margaret. So, I'm actually learning from her. She's absolutely brilliant at it and that, I think, is going to be my next step.

Nicola: Well that would be great, especially if you're going to be, presumably, putting some kind of roots down. So what are you looking forward to in the next year or so?

Jeni: Well, I'm really excited about this, the new project that we are launching, Brilliant, Etc. I think it is going to help millions of people around the world. One of the things I said on the website, in the documentary, was that this is the first time in history where every person on the planet has the opportunity to have a voice. You think about the history in England and how far back it goes and everything everybody has gone through. This really is the first time, the first time, that everyone has this opportunity. How empowering is that? So, I'm really hoping that I can be the one to, not only provide the tools and the resources for that, but the inspiration that it is possible that you can do this.

Nicola: Well you've had an amazing impact on the people that you spoke for at the NPO World Summit and we're going to put a link to that video underneath your podcast episode just because you quietly stood on the stage and just blew everyone in the room away. It was really quite impressive to watch.

Jeni: Thank you.

Nicola: Good stuff. Doing the whole university, the blogging course for universities, you've got Brilliantetc. com and I really wish you well and I hope to meet you one day in person and thank you very much for spending time with us today.

Jeni: Thank you, it's been an absolute pleasure.

Nicola: All right. Bye Jenni.

Jeni: Buh bye.

Visit Jeni at BrilliantEtc.com

3. DAN NORRIS

Nicola : Hi, it's Nicola Cairncross, and today I'm so delighted to be joined by Dan Norris, whose book has had a tremendous impact over on this side of the pond when it was released just recently. Dan is an award winning content marketer and the author of the bestselling business book The 7 Day Startup. If you haven't read it and you're interested in business, go and get it now. It's amazing. In June 2014, after failing at entrepreneurship for seven years, he founded WPCurve.com, a worldwide team of WordPress developers providing unlimited small fixed and support 24/7 for $69 a month. It became profitable in just 23 days and 14 months later has 21 staff, 500 customers, and continues to grow at 15-20% a month.

Dan is a passionate content marketer and has created 600 plus pieces of content around entrepreneurship, WordPress, and online marketing. In 2013, he was voted Australia's best small business blogger by the readers of Telstra's Smarter Business Ideas magazine. In 2014, Dan released his book The 7 Day Startup, which became a top 10 bestseller in three Amazon categories, and I know personally has changed the life of entrepreneurs across the globe. Welcome to the call, Dan. How are you?

Dan Norris: I'm very good. I'm a bit flattered after that intro.

Nicola: No, it totally is true. I can't remember how it came on my radar. I think my sister Sarah alerted me to it. She was reading it and she was in the middle of trying to get something going and it just had such tremendous effect on her. I bought it as well and read it in a weekend.

The clarity. I honestly think it's the best book since the Lean Startup books for new and aspiring entrepreneurs.

Dan Norris: That's very nice of you to say. I really wasn't sure when I pulled the trigger to put it up there. I really had absolutely no idea whether anyone was going to grab it. What's happened since has been a big surprise.

Nicola: I'm sure. Let's go back. Let's go back. Obviously I've read your story in the book, but I want you to share with my listeners in 84 countries now how you became an entrepreneur, what kind of background you came from, and how you got through all those years when it just wasn't working. Tell us all about you.

Dan Norris: You've mentioned the seven years of running my previous business, which was a web agency. I think I probably wanted to be an entrepreneur a long time before that. Probably another six years before that when I was at university, but I didn't launch anything. I kind of came up with ideas reasonably often and I did subjects at university and did planning and that kind of thing, but I didn't actually launch anything. 2006 it was, when I was 26, I was working in a good job and I always thought I would be an entrepreneur at some stage, so I decided that that was the time and I left a very good job where I was getting paid very well, I didn't have to work all that hard, I was getting a promotion just about every year, and I didn't really have anything to go to. Luckily, I had a wife who was earning an income and we could get by if everything went really, really bad.

I just left and I started building websites for people and I just slaved away at that for seven years. Just could never really make it work. I was always able to make enough to pay a really small wage, but I was never able to grow it really significantly. Even in year seven, I wasn't making any more profit than I was making in year one. It was just making more revenue, but more money, more problems type thing.

Nicola: This is really interesting for me because I've just started a Facebook Ads agency, but before that, for about the last four years,

I've been running a done for you digital marketing agency. I found some of the stories in the book about this time you experienced were very telling. The constant chasing after new clients, the clients' expectations, etc., etc. A lot of people are selling this as an opportunity for Internet marketers to start their own web agency. Tell us what you experienced because I think it will be a salient true tell for people.

Dan Norris: What I experienced isn't exactly what everyone else experienced, but I know it is a very, very common thing because a lot of the people in my audience had come on board over the years running very similar businesses and having the same struggles. Every time I write one of these posts about that experience, I always get a bunch of replies of people telling me, "Yeah, I know exactly what you mean because I've gone through it." Yeah, it's just basically comes back to a fundamental problem of the business relying too much on you and you not having that consistency, reliability of income, and that scalability of something ... If you think about a software startup, they're just infinitely scalable. They can just keep growing, sign up more customers. It's just a technical problem that needs to be solved.

With an agency, they're just not really scalable by nature. They're extremely difficult to scale. What I wanted to do was bring the aspects of the software scalability into the services area, which is what I did with WP Curve. Before I saw some success with that, I tried everything else you can possibly think of with the agency to make it work. It just kept running into brick walls. Every time I hired someone, it would just put my costs up and make things more stressful. Every time I took on a big project, it would require more of my time. I tried to take on a lot of smaller projects instead so I can get people to do the work, but then I just couldn't get enough of the projects to grow it to a decent scale.

They're also local in nature, which limits the market size and they're extremely competitive and very hard to differentiate. There's just so many issues to running an agency.

Nicola: I recognized all of them.

Dan Norris: Make it difficult.

Nicola: It was painful to read your tales of pivoting slightly to look for new markets and things. I just related to it so much. Then you've got the clients who want to pay nothing to get leads that are worth a fortune to them, and then you've got the fact that they want to [own 00:08:16] you up with the top person because they perceive that's the only person who's got any skills. It just goes on, really, doesn't it?

Dan Norris: I think you need to be a little bit ruthless to run an agency well. What I always struggled with was how do I come up with a reasonable price and a reasonable level of service and a reasonable amount of availability? I struggled with that. How available do I have to be to a client who's paying me $10,000 for a big project? Do I have to give up my Christmas holiday, which I did twice, for this client? Eventually, do I fire this client? Which I did, which had a massive impact on my business because they're about a quarter of my whole business. The way I dealt with that, there's a lot of ways you could deal with that. You could just be a ruthless person. A lot of agency owners are. Or you could hire someone. You can have really strict rules.

The way I dealt with it is just by having a really simple service. With WP Curve, I don't have to have any of those conversations because we've got a very clear offering and it's either a yes or a now generally.

Nicola: What my first business coach called a Salford close. Salford's a very tough area of Manchester. He said, "If you could just imagine yourself standing there ready to head butt someone and say, "Do you want it or what then?" That's called the Salford close."

Dan Norris: Right. I was never very good at sales either, so that was part of my working out how to get by in business without being good at sales, which I guess we'll get into later.

Nicola: Tell me a bit about your background. What kind of family do you come from? Are they entrepreneurs or are you the strange chip off the block as it were?

Dan Norris: Not really. My grandfather owned racehorses and owned businesses for most of his life. I guess it got passed down from there. My dad was sort of a business guy, accountant and manager, CEO type guy. I remember being in the careers counselor at school and asked me what I wanted to do and I just said, "Business," and he said, "Why?" I said, "I don't know, because my dad's a businessman." In terms of entrepreneurship, there wasn't that much entrepreneurship in my life growing up. I think my drive to be an entrepreneur came more out of just personal boredom and inability to work for someone else.

Nicola: Yeah, relate to that as well.

Dan Norris: Just the creation aspect. When you're an entrepreneur, you can just create things on a daily basis that are things you decide you want to create. It's kind of hard to get a job that allows you to do that, so you have to create that for yourself.

Nicola: That's interesting, isn't it, that it's not very valued in corporate life, because it's the one thing ... I read a book by the guy who ran Hallmark Cards, or he was ... Damn, I can't remember. It had an amazing illustration on the front of it about spinning out around the world because Hallmark has somehow managed to attract top creative talent and keep them, and that's apparently quite a difficult thing for a corporate to attract and keep creative people, because the ...

Dan Norris: I think you need to feel like you've got the ability to change things, and if you don't feel that, then you're not going to be inspired as a creative person. It's very, very difficult to have that environment in a big company.

Nicola: That's very true. The racehorses, that's an entrepreneur right there, isn't it? Anyone who gets involved in betting and racing.

Dan Norris: Yeah, that's right. There is a bit of a gambling aspect to it.

Nicola: Okay, you're running the agency. It's gradually dawning on you that while it's working ... That's a double edged sword, isn't it? If something works a bit, enough just to bring in some money and then it takes you a while to realize it's not going to be scalable, as you say. Then how did your thought process go then? Did you immediately start thinking, "I've got to find something that's software based?" Did you meet someone who gave you the idea? What happened?

Dan Norris: I was very, very indecisive, very noncommittal. I tried everything I could to avoid making what was a really hard decision. I'd gotten as far as being able to live on the coast in a good area, which wasn't in the city. We'd moved there. We had kids and things weren't great, but they were okay. If I was to give up my business and have to get a job, then that was going to compromise all of that. It was a very, very difficult decision to make and it took me a long time to make it. Way too long, but eventually I just decided, again, to follow the same behavior from before and just throw myself in the deep end. I figured it worked when I left my job.

This time, the stakes were a bit higher because I had a family. I ended up selling my business for, I think it was about 70 grand or something like that. That gave me about a year. I had that year to work on something that I deemed would be able to grow into something that was more scalable. Software was what I was thinking initially, and if I wasn't going to do it after that year, then I would have been pretty much screwed.

Nicola: A year with being paid and not having to go to work, not having all those extra added stresses. That's bound to help the creativity a bit, isn't it?

Dan Norris: Yeah. I had a very productive career in that I had a lot of success with my content compared to anything I'd done before. I sort of started to build a bit of a story that people would follow along with and I got more involved in the community of entrepreneurs. There was a lot of positives from that point of view. From the business point of view, there was just a constant pressure of hoping this thing was going to work and waiting for it to kick in and waiting for it to start working, but it just never came. There was just that stress of knowing that eventually this is going to run out and eventually it became pretty obvious that it wasn't going to work.

Nicola: What were you working on at that time then?

Dan Norris: It was a software app. I had three or four different ideas I could work on, and I just picked the least worst one.

Nicola: By whose criteria?

Dan Norris: I kind of picked one that I'd already built and used to some extent. It was a dashboard for analytics, so it talked to your different software programs: Google Analytics, MailChimp, that kind of thing. Zero accounting, and it brought in your analytics into the one spot. That idea itself had been done before, but I just wanted to make it really simple, like a dashboard for small business people who don't really understand analytics. They just want to get simple stats. I spent a lot of time doing what I thought was validating the idea, but really I think it was just procrastinating and not doing the work that I needed to do, which was to figure out a way to launch it as fast as possible. Eventually, I think I got to 11 and a half months and I had 10 signups and $470 in monthly revenue. I was paying around 1500 a month, at least, just to keep it going with my developers and everything else, and I was two weeks away from running out of money and having to get a job. That's when I decided I needed to make a change.

Nicola: Yeah. That really struck home when I read that, because I thought, Blimey, he was really up against it there. How did the idea for WP Curve come? I believe it wasn't called that, originally.

Dan Norris: No. I think I'd probably been thinking about the idea before that two week period, because it's sort of right in my wheelhouse of expertise in terms of supporting business owners with websites. It's not that much of a revolutionary idea. It's just doing it in a way that is more of a scalable way because it's a fixed price service and it's a recurring service. It's got a bit of a twist in terms of it being live and only small jobs. I'm not sure where I got the idea for the live, the 24/7 live thing. Again, it doesn't feel like a revolutionary idea. I'm sure someone else before me thought of having a developer who's always there.

I knew a lot of people on my email list had problems with their site and I was always told about the pain of dealing with agencies. I'd experienced it firsthand. I'd experience horror in people. I know I'd ask in Elance firsthand and the problems with that. I knew there was something in between. I just had no idea what it was and I really had no choice to stuff around working at if it was a good idea. I just had to launch it as quickly as possible. That's what I did. I sent an email to my list and called it WP Live Ninja and I set up a live chat app on my phone. That just said this service is, I think I said, $50 a month or something and you can get 24/7 access to my web developer. When I went to bed at night, I'd have my phone on live chat, so if it went off I'd jump on there and be the support desk!

Nicola: I'll bet your wife loved that.

Dan Norris: Yeah, I just told her it wouldn't last forever, but it lasted for about three months until I met my co-founder Alex, and he started in the US and started looking after that side of the world, so that made things easier.

Nicola: Oh, okay, yes. You're carving up the globe between you.

Dan Norris: Yeah. It was actually quite funny because after a week of launching WP Curve, I had exactly $476 in monthly recurring revenue, and that was the exact same amount that I had after one year of running the analytics dashboard. I thought that was a bit of an omen.

Nicola: Yeah, absolutely. The signs were there, weren't they? Success leads process, as they say. Where do I start with my questions? Right. I've got a best friend, Steve Watson, who is a WordPress developer. He takes people's websites and moves them onto WordPress and he does lovely designs and all that stuff. From his point of view, it's not economically viable for him to do little jobs. He's now introduced to attention things for his previous clients where he can do X number of jobs for them over the month, because there is constant little adjustments. There's plugins to be updated, there's themes to be updated, there's you want changes done but you're not confident to do them yourself. As a business owner, you're always terrified you're going to break your website, aren't you?

Dan Norris: Yeah. Yeah, exactly.

Nicola: It made absolute sense when I read about it. I suppose to your clients, it obviously made absolute sense and they just signed up.

Dan Norris: Yeah. I'd also built a decent audience over that time. Unfortunately, because I'd sold the other business, I wasn't in contact with any of the clients from that business after I'd sold it. I'd built an email list through the analytics dashboard and all this content I put out. I think I was really starting to get some momentum with that content. It was under a completely different name and a completely different website, but I still had my email list and I was emailing every week. I had a forum of entrepreneurs which I was active in. I had a bit of something to kick it off, which really helped, and it kicked that momentum into place, and that's just literally gone on day after day, week after week, month after month. Today was crazy. We hired two people. We've had about 12 signups. It continues to be crazy.

Nicola: It must be the kind of service that people refer to their friends. It's just so easy to refer business, isn't it? it's simple to talk about.

Dan Norris: Yeah. I like to think it's all of my amazing content that drives all the leads, but in reality it's probably got very little to do with it. It's probably just people use the service and they and their friends have had this problem for a long time, and this service comes in somewhere between an agency and a marketplace of developers, and gives them a certain level of quality for a reasonable price and it's easy for them to tell people about.

Nicola: I've experienced the whole Elance thing. I didn't use it for years because I was convinced that, A, nobody could do it as well as me, which is absolute nonsense, and B, I didn't know how to choose good people. Then I actually met someone who was an Elance poster boy and used them all the time, and he taught me how to put a job on Elance properly and weed out all the responses. A lot of people are absolutely terrified, and rightly so, to hire the wrong person because it could be expensive, it can take forever, and then they can screw up what you've already got. It is a worry for people, isn't it?

Dan Norris: Yeah. The way I think about things like this in my business now is so different to the way I used to think about it because now we've got a business that's doing a good amount of revenue. We can pay for services without thinking twice about them. If they solve a problem, we'll pay for them. We won't sit there and worry about the cost. Now my day is more about how can I possibly figure out a way to do less? [inaudible 00:21:11] too much stuff to do. I think there's a lot of businesses like that out there, where they just couldn't think of anything worse than getting onto the marketplaces and trying to figure out a way to hire someone for one little job.

Nicola: I was talking today James Schramko recently. I asked him what his goal for 2015 was, and he said to become the absolute best surfer I can. That sums it up.

Dan Norris: [crosstalk 00:21:34] I've been down to see James a couple of times and I haven't yet been surfing with him.

Nicola: That is true, isn't it? Once you reach a certain level in business, it's not about saving a penny here and there all the time and doing all the work yourself. It is literally freeing up the time from doing the recurring jobs so that you can think better. Thinking is probably your highest and best use now, isn't it, of your time?

Dan Norris: Possibly. I don't tend to prioritize things like surfing. I'm not coming to it from that point of view, but I'm more coming at it from the point of view of there's a bunch of things that I need to do within the team, whether it's motivating the team or talking to them or whatever. I think I've got 10 or 15 people that I'm overseeing directly now, and then add in everything else you've got to do as a parent and business partner, and then add in all the content, and we just hired a new guy to do the content. There's always really high priority stuff that needs to be done. If we're looking at can we get a service or a piece of software to just save us a few minutes a day, if me and Alex can do that, then we do that. Not thinking that it'll mean we don't have to work. It'll just mean we can work on stuff that's a bit more important.

Nicola: Yeah. I think what James meant is he has his best ideas away from the computer, so that's what he's focusing on, getting away from that.

Dan Norris: No, he just doesn't want to work.

Nicola: Oh my goodness. Let's just go back a little bit now. You've launched the business. It's making more in a month than your other business did in several years. You've got a feeling you're onto something here. Fast forward six months down the line. How did you start to grow it?

Dan Norris: We really just hit this momentum where, for one thing, the business is structured in a way, like you do with a software company. It's a simple formula where it has to grow each month if you have more people signing up than those leaving. We had a really simple equation. We had, I think, 10 people in the first week. I think there was maybe 25 people in the first month sign up. Literally all we had to do for month two was make sure that we got more people signing up than those 25 and we kept as many of the 25 as possible. When you structure a business like that, it's kind of easy to grow it. If it's got to that position where you've got that fit there and already started paying for it and telling people about it.

Everything we did from that point just boosted that momentum. We did things really gradually. We solved problems as we had them. For example, the live chat thing, I didn't solve that problem until I needed to, until I was getting woken up three or four times a night [crosstalk 00:24:35] once a week. We ran on email only, just in Gmail, a shared support box until that didn't work as a help desk system. I ran with one developer until the response time wasn't acceptable, so we got another developer and another developer. We ran with WP Live Ninja and the template I put together in an hour or two until we were in a good position to build a nicer site. We just did it that way, and every time we leveled up, it created a boost in our conversion.

When we went from the old WP Curve site to a new design, that really boosted our conversion. When I signed up Alex and I was able to focus more on content myself, that really boosted things. When we got the help desk system ... Sort of everything we did from there really boosted that momentum. The content in particular started going really well. I don't think there's anything specifically that we did. I think I'd just been doing it for quite a while before that. I just kept doing what I was doing. I kind of learnt what works. This month, I think we had 50,000 people to our site, which was way more than we had a year ago. I think a year ago, we were getting about 5,000 people a month to the site. Just every month, it's gone up and up and up.

Same as the book. It started out as an idea. We kind of built on it. I wrote a bunch of blog posts, and eventually it just got a life of its own and grew into this thing that it is now. I guess what we've done is we've done things slowly, but when we're seeing good results, we've kept doing the same thing and just followed that momentum.

Nicola: The book started as a series of blogs posts. Did you get good responses from those, which made you think you were perhaps onto something? Do you read a lot of other business books?

Dan Norris: No, I don't read much at all. I haven't read many business books. I've read The Lean Startup. It took me about four goes, because it's the most boring thing I've ever ready, but it was obviously very influential, and I ended up reading it via audio if that's how you say it because I just couldn't get through it. I'm absolutely hopeless at reading books. I'm pretty good at listening to podcasts. I listen to lots of podcasts. I guess in terms of traction, it's kind of funny. I've released virtually every word from this book before I launched the book. I put almost all the content up on my own site or some other people's sites. I volunteered to about 20 different podcasts to talk about each chapter. I sent key parts of the book, like all the pretend marketing ideas, posts off to different websites. Some of them didn't want them to publish them.

Some of it got really good traction. Some of it got really bad traction. I put some up on Facebook. The intro to the book came because I was just having a random thought about when I was on my honeymoon and I read Think and Grow Rich, and I convinced myself I was going to be a millionaire. I put that on Facebook, and I just got loads of likes on that update, so I thought, that's obviously appealing to people, so I'll use that as the intro to the book. Yeah, it was kind of like what's getting traction, what's not getting traction. Also just personal motivation because I find it quite easy to write a blog post, but I thought I'd probably struggle to write a whole book without getting some kind of validation as I went that it was actually useful.

Plus, I only intended to write it to have an opt in on my site, just as a giveaway. I just thought, imagine I'll just give all the content away and just put it out in blog posts. If I'm going to give it away as a PDF anyway, I might as well just give it away now. After I spent so long on going back and forth with the editing and the formatting, and I kind of looked at it and I'm like, "Man, that looks pretty nice. It kind of looks like a business book. I should actually make an effort with the marketing."

Nicola: Yeah, it's interesting. I wrote my first book as a series of 101 emails. Because I realized I needed a follow-up sequence. This was back in 2000, 2001, something like that. I was following someone who was using one shopping cart to send out auto emails, and I thought, that's pretty cool, let's do that. Then I realized I needed to plan it all out. Otherwise, I'd never do it. Then when I got to day 15, I realized I'd better get some people in it or I'd never finish it. I had a bunch of people following along. That kept me doing writing the daily emails to a pre-determined plan of content. I would never have done it if I hadn't got those people in, and you're right. They gave me feedback and asked questions and made it easier to make it clearer. I highly recommend this way of writing books in chunks. It's much easier.

Dan Norris: I did a similar thing. I originally thought I'd put a business growth course on the site. It's funny you mention Schramko because I've consumed a lot of his content over the years and I've known him for a while. I think I was checking out one of his courses, Wealthification or something like that. It was full of useful high level strategies for business growth, but I really wanted something that I could have given myself when I was running my agency that told me exactly what I needed to do. Not general strategy, but "This is why your business is not growing, and these are some of the features of businesses that do grow and this is how to build those features into your own."

I started writing what I thought would be either a video email course or just an email course on the site. The more I wrote, I kind of just put the ideas in Trello and started writing some of these ideas and picking up some old blog posts I've written and things like this. Before I knew it, I just had so much content that it actually became the book ... I was planning on writing a book anyway, but it wasn't going to be about this. This is the content that just came so easily and eventually, it just ... The actual writing of the first draft of the book only took me a couple of days. I just went home, sat outside, and just typed all of this out. The editing took forever, but the first draft of actually writing the content was really quick because it just came out so easily.

Nicola: You mentioned Trello there, which is a project management tool that is recommended for creative people, isn't it?

Dan Norris: Yeah, I've been using it just for gathering my ideas. I was using Evernote at one point for notes, but I just found it really hard to just manage the structure of ideas.

Nicola: Yes. I'm not getting on with it either.

Dan Norris: Yeah. Trello's cool for books. It's free. I think I had four or five different ideas for books that I could have worked on, so I set up a board with four or five different lists, and I put all of the key topics on each list as a task or a card. Then I looked at the one that had the most on it and the one I was frequently updating because that's where all of my ideas were, and this one just really stood out as being the one to go with. Eventually I moved from that and just put it in a Google doc and just started writing it all.

Nicola: Tell us, before we move into your business mind, marketing, and money, tell us about The 7 Day Startup. When I first came across you, it was quite early in the process of you releasing it. What's happened since then? Tell us the story of The 7 Day Startup.

Dan Norris: I did put it up for free, because that's what I told everyone I would do, and I wanted to do that because I didn't think anyone would read it, so I wanted to put it out for free. I did that, and I actually hired a guy, Tom [Mawkes 00:32:06], it was just, again, a random course of events where we put a blog post out requesting people to express an interest in being an intern for WP Curve, to look after our content. Tom's application really impressed me, but he didn't get the position because i found someone who just after all was a slightly better fit.

I just emailed Tom and said, "Man, I've written this book. I was just going to chuck it up on my site or put it up on Amazon if I could figure out how to do that. I don't know if you know anything about book marketing, but if you can Google a bunch of blog posts and figure out how we can market this book, then I'll just pay you for one month. You can just be my intern for one month," because the other guy wasn't going to start for a month, "And we can do that." He's like, "All right, cool, yes, I'd love to work with you." It turns out he's got a publishing company and he knows everything about marketing books. It was just a really weird thing. I think when I emailed him, I didn't even really know that or remember that, because we got over 100 applications, and I was just wary from looking at them all.

He just went for it. I chatted to him. We came up with a huge list of things to do, who the influencers were. He came up with the idea of getting a group of ambassadors together in a Facebook group and an email list, and he built a landing page. Just worked constantly for that three week period. He created the listing on Amazon, worked with the format. I think we only finished it the day before we actually uploaded it to Amazon.

Nicola: Yeah, deadlines are wonderful things.

Dan Norris: Yeah. It was lucky because I was presenting the day before it was ready in Wordcamp in Sydney and I was like, "Ah yes, my book'll be available tomorrow." Some guy's like, "Actually, I just put it on Amazon. It's available right now." I'm like, "Oh cool, I didn't know that, but that's nice."

Nicola: Then everyone went and bought it immediately, which must have given a nice little boost.

Dan Norris: No no, I told them not to, because I said, "Don't worry, it's going to be free tomorrow," but it was up there for like $1 or something and I just said, "We'll just wait for it to go free." The ambassador group was really useful and a lot of those guys got on there and left reviews on Amazon. It just took off. The surprising thing, I think in the first week it got 12,000 downloads when it was free. It hit number one in most of the categories it was in, like startups and small business and entrepreneurship.

Then I thought, when we moved it to paid, which is something I had to do, I would have just left it free, except Amazon make you move it to paid. I never thought I would make any money on this book because I'd been told by everyone that you never make money writing books. We moved it to paid and I just expected it to drop off, because it's one thing getting to the free listings, but getting to rank in the paid listings, I thought, was just going to be an impossibility. It just continued to rank. I think it's still number two in startups and number three in small businesses, something like that. It's never beaten Peter Thiel's book so far. That's the only one it hasn't beaten yet. Yeah, it's still getting 50 to 70 or 80 purchases a day.

Nicola: That's amazing.

Dan Norris: Has been since about six weeks ago when it went off being free, or whenever that happened.

Nicola: It's such a wonderful feeling, isn't it, to look at a page on Amazon and see your book in the listings?

Dan Norris: Yeah. I don't know if you follow me on Facebook, but I was updating it every day going, "Wow, look at this. This is amazing." People must have gotten really sick of it. I normally just put pictures of beer, so it was probably a nice change.

Nicola: The thing I really liked about it, as someone who, I've written three books now and read a lot more. I'm an avid reader, [strobe 00:35:48] listener now. The thing I loved about it was the combination of your story, which really drew us in, instructions on what to do, and the really practical how to stuff. You manage to tell people how to do things like installing a WordPress website in half a page. It was just astonishingly economical. It was efficient. It was an economical and efficient book, but inspiring at the same time. There's not many books that can do the two together.

Dan Norris: I'm usually pretty good at writing how to stuff, but this story component ... I think I'm okay at telling my own story, but at the same time, but I don't read a lot of books. I don't think I'm really much of a writer. I don't really know how to structure a good story and how to make it flow well and all that kind of stuff that writers do. It's kind of a bit of a mystery to me. I had an editor who just went through and cleaned it up. I don't really even know exactly what she did, but I know it took her a long time, and I know that by the time she was finished it was a lot better than what it was when I gave it to her. That's a bit of a mystery. Yeah, I think she did a really good job of making sure it flowed well and that the stories were told in the right places. Of course, all of the general stuff that editors do like consistency in fixing typos [crosstalk 00:37:18]

Nicola: Grammar and spelling and stuff, yes.

Dan Norris: That was the girl from Writing Business Well. Writing Business Well was the name of her first site. She's got a podcast called Writers' Rough Drafts, which I've been listening to a lot because she interviews writers. They're just generally interesting people, so if people are looking for tips on writing, then that's a cool thing to listen to.

Nicola: What doors has it opened? Having a successful book like this.

Dan Norris: I wasn't really looking for it to open any doors because there's nothing, really, that I'm interested in doing other than exactly what I'm doing at the moment. I've presented at a few conferences, but I'm kind of on the fence about whether or not I'll do that again because it's highly stressful to me and it's not really that enjoyable, going to conferences without presenting. It's hard work.

Nicola: Yeah, it can be scary. That's for sure.

Dan Norris: I've had some amazing stuff happen in terms of people emailing me. I've got a Facebook group now with 8 or 900 members. We've had a huge growth in the business over the last six weeks. I've had people contacting me, podcasters like Pat Flynn and just people running startup conferences and all kinds of stuff that I just never would've ever expected would happen.

Nicola: Opportunities. I listened to your Pat Flynn ... I'm a big fan of Pat. Been following him for a long time. If anyone's listening and you use WordPress, that is a not to be missed podcast because you give us 10 tips on how to improve your use of WordPress, don't you?

Dan Norris: Yeah, and I also have started replying to the comments on his sit and I think we're up to about 400 comments, so if you want to go check out his site. I've told people I'd give them three or four things to improve on their site, thinking maybe 50, 60 people might reply, but 400. There's about 100 I haven't replied to.

Nicola: Are you having to outsource that or you're doing it all yourself?

Dan Norris: No way. No. That's part of the fun. That's the stuff I like doing. I just do the stuff I like doing and I can outsource the stuff I don't like doing.

Nicola: Yeah, and that's great because it's giving you insights into what are the problems people are having.

Dan Norris: It's funny, actually. A lot of the stuff is really, I'm just writing a lot of the same stuff over and over and over again, and to me just seems really obvious, really simple things. Obviously, it's still things that a lot of people struggle with. I don't know, maybe I'll write a blog post at the end of it and summarize all of the common things and how to fix them.

Nicola: Those Top 10 blog posts, they get so much traction, don't they? Only day before yesterday I got a mention in the Huffington Post because I'd written my top 10 business books. It's now expanded to top 25.

Dan Norris: Nice.

Nicola: I know. I nearly fell off my chair when the Google Alert came in. You can imagine.

Dan Norris: That's very cool.

Nicola: Bloggers like Nicola Cairn, I was like, hang on a minute. I'm the only blogger they've mentioned. What's going on?

Dan Norris: That's very cool. Yeah. I think that's mostly good. People say that they're linkbaity or whatever or they're too standard or whatever, but I like to have the structure when I write a blog post and I like to have a way of forming a decent size post for people. The list post is just a real easy way to do that. When I started creating content, I used to go to the big sites that I was competing with in terms of attention, like Copyblogger and Hubspot or whatever, and I'd look at the content that was doing really well. All of them were list posts. It was always 15 things to do, top 10 X, whatever. I think it doesn't hurt to do the occasional list post either.

Nicola: No, it doesn't. They're certainly not being penalized by Google. That's for sure, because I get loads of traffic for my list posts I did back in 2010, 2011. Good. Let's transition now into what you've learnt along the way. Would like to know about Your Business Mind Marketing, and Money.

Nicola: What would you like to tell an aspiring entrepreneur just getting started about the business mind and how yours has changed and what you've learned?

Dan Norris: I think the main thing for me is I see a lot of people creating businesses, but I don't see that many people creating something that can really be a really big business. I think the change that I made in my mind was going from I want to be a business person, which really in practice meant I want to work for myself, to I want to create a startup. When you decide to create a startup, you're not doing it for the purpose of creating a job for yourself. You're doing something that is in a big market, something that can scale, something that would maybe one day appear on a big tech press site or a business magazine because it's captured that much attention that it's relevant to so many people.

I think that kind of thing can be done by someone who doesn't have a lot of funding, and that's what we're trying to do with WP Curve so far. I've seen other people do it. I don't think it's easy to do without funding, but I think it's possible. The starting point is realizing how big the opportunity is. I think in most things, unless you're doing some little niche project, in most things there's an opportunity out there that's far, far bigger than you realize if you're willing to figure out how to make it appeal to the whole world or a huge group of people, not just a local business.

Nicola: Yeah. A lot of people think that startups, you have to go on that whole startup, venture capital, present ... I did it back in 2000 or so. I had a little startup called ArtistManager.com, which was a database driven site that matched up people who turned up for X Factor auditions with managers who were looking for new artists. Because I'd been a manager and my artist had suddenly decided they didn't want to do music anymore. They wanted to do video, and I thought, where do I find a new artist fast? I went on the whole venture capital thing and presenting to bit teams of VCs, and it was absolutely terrifying. I think people have got this idea in their mind that startups have to be funded and you have to go through a year or two of pitching to investors, but you've proved that it can be done on a shoestring.

Dan Norris: Yeah, and there's examples in my book of people who started up without funding. There's plenty of other examples that have gone on to get funding. In fact, one of the examples I use in my book Bare Metrics, when I spoke to Josh, I think he'd only been going for about six months. He'd just launched it himself. He'd launched it in one week. It was a little software analytics app, and the most painful thing about it is it was, in a way, quite similar to the app I built and totally failed at. He did things a lot better than I did. He just announced half a million dollars in funding a couple of weeks after I brought the book out. I can't remember the valuation, but I think it was a $10 million evaluation, or something that was a very big number for one guy working on his own software app.

There are examples our there of people who, when they build something, they do it at such a level of quality that it gets notice. Even though Informly failed, I was able to get noticed with it. I did get a bit of attention from investors. I got covered in the tech press like Mashable and Nextweb and places like that and local startup press. I think when you can execute something well and you can tap into a market that is much bigger than a local business, it's possible to position yourself as a startup even if you're not a funded company.

Nicola: Yeah, absolutely. There's two stages, isn't there? There's before you even do anything, get startup money. Then there's the thing where you're actually proving that there's a need in the marketplace, and that's when investors get interested as well, isn't it, when you're starting to get some traction?

Dan Norris: The whole investor thing is a little confusing, I think, to a lot of people. I think it depends a lot on where you live and what circles you run in. Where I'm from, I'm in a co-working space right now and they've got an incubator going. It's not the sort of thing that you get funding at the end of. It's not the sort of thing that they take equity in. It's just come here and learn about business. That's a very, very different environment to my co-founder, who's in San Francisco. Every single guy there has a company [crosstalk 00:46:34] coffee shop's got a coffee startup. I don't know if you've seen Silicon Valley, the TV show, but apparently it's just like that.

Nicola: No I haven't, but I've listened to Walter and [Yaro 00:46:43]. They're entrepreneurs. Everything Entrepreneurship podcast, and Yaro's a typical Internet marketer, infomarketer, lifestyle business, and Walter's actually over in San Francisco at the moment. I think Yaro's heading over there because he's very drawn to that whole environment. It does sound very exciting, I must say.

Dan Norris: That's funny. Is that Yaro Starak?

Nicola: Yes.

Dan Norris: I'm guessing there's only one Yaro. He actually lives quite close to me. I've never met him. I probably should.

Nicola: He's about to move to San Francisco, so you'll have to make it quick.

Dan Norris: Actually, I think he might actually be a customer. That's funny. Maybe I should!

Nicola: Listen to their podcast, Everything Entrepreneurship. They don't do it very often. There's one about every three weeks, but they catch up with what both of them have been doing and they're very good friends. They joke amongst themselves. It's a very listenable podcast, but they do compare notes on the different worlds they work in, and I find it absolutely fascinating.

Dan Norris: It is really interesting. He's been on my radar for a long time because I heard about him mentioned back when I first got into following these Internet marketing guys. Yeah, it's really interesting, the guys who've upgraded. They're just selling their $9 info products and running the big multi million dollar software startups. A few guys have done that in that community. I think the priorities really change and the stuff they talk about really changes and the way they approach things and people that hang out really changes. I like to follow the startup world, even though I don't have any intention of moving over there or getting funding. Their way of thinking is more in line with my way of thinking.

Nicola: It's much bitter, isn't it? I live near around Brighton in England, and they call that Silicon Beach, because that's where the main hub apart from London is for tech startups in the UK. I keep saying, keep meaning I must get out and network more often because there's quite a lot of things, coffee mornings and things for startup entrepreneurs. It's a very exciting ... It makes you think differently, and I think that's really important. Think bigger.

Dan Norris: Yeah. That's funny, because we've got a Silicon Beach here, which I'm assuming stole it from you guys.

Nicola: I don't know about that. There's quite a bit more sand, that's for sure.

Dan Norris: If you want to sue anyone, I can put you onto the people who are responsible.

Nicola: It's a bit of a joke, really, because Brighton Beach is covered in pebbles, not sand, and it's nothing like as gorgeous as your beaches in Australia. I think it's bit of a British ironic twist on that one.

Dan Norris: Just on the topic of thinking bigger, the reason it happened to me, I think, is because I started listening to This Week in Startups. It's a show about startups by a guy who's just lived in this startup world his whole life. I remember he got the guys from Base Camp on and he referred to their business as a lifestyle business. This is a business doing multiple millions of dollars a year and has millions of customers. He's like, "Ah, you know, you got a nice little lifestyle business there." That really changed my mind. Every week he's got a different company on, like this dog vacay ... I got an email this morning that they've raised $25 million and Home Joy, who did cleaning, had raised $37 million.

All these companies where I'm sure everyone listening to this show at one point has thought of starting a business like this. Like, I'll look after your dog when you're on holidays or I'll clean your house or whatever. They just haven't gone that extra step of saying a very big percent of the world has a dog. A very big percentage of the world needs their house cleaned. How can you build something that maybe starts small but maybe you build something that's appealing and a brand that's appealing worldwide. Then you might start getting noticed by people in other areas and investors and a community that can refer you to customers and all that kind of stuff. I think that's probably my biggest tip there.

Nicola: I would love to talk startup all day, but something popped into my head, that we got a company called TrustedHousesitters.com. Based out of Brighton, and basically they hook up people all around the world with houses that need looking after, with people who are willing to go and stay in those houses for free and look after the houses and stray pets. You can do it for two weeks or a month or six months or whatever. They're just growing at a phenomenal rate. Again, it's one of those things that they start on a shoestring and then it's getting traction. I want to know more about you.

Dan Norris: Things like Airbnb, these billion dollar companies that are just doing the exact same things. All these markets are huge and people often don't actually realize how big they are.

Nicola: Yeah, absolutely. Let's find out more about your business mind though, fascinating as this is. What else have you learned about yourself as an entrepreneur and a business person?

Dan Norris: That's really the main thing. I don't analyze the way I think too much, except that I try to create a lot of value and I don't think too much about whether I'm getting immediately rewarded for that value. I think that's something that's paid off for me. From the beginning of starting this company, I wanted to start something big and something that was going to have a big impact and something that was scalable. I suppose that's always influenced my thinking around the decisions that we make.

At every stage of running this business, there's been opportunities to do 1,000 different things and we've turned down work day after day after day, but I've always come back to the fact that we are focused on launching something really big. I guess it's a bit of a strong willedness or whatever the word is where we're able to say no to stuff because we've learnt that we're after a bigger market. It might take a bigger time. Strong willed enough to say no to that stuff. That's been my way I think.

Nicola: Yeah, going after just a bigger market with a simple offer. The simplicity and focus in everything you do stands out a mile, which is really interesting. Tell me about your business marketing, then. How big was your list when you started? You had a bit of traction. You had an audience, and you had a list. How big was that list at that time?

Dan Norris: I think when I started the analytics dashboard, I had about 1500 people on the list. Email lists go stale very quickly.

Nicola: They do, don't they?

Dan Norris: Yeah. 1500 sounds like a lot, but when I used to send an email, I'd be lucky to get two or three replies. I knew there was a couple of people on there that would read the emails and maybe I had a 20% open rate or something, but it wasn't huge by any means. I think at the end of Informly and before I started WP Curve, it was probably up to 4 or 5,000, and I think now it's up to like 13 or 14,000 or something like that.

Nicola: You haven't got the 50,000, 100,000 list that some people listening might think you had. It was relatively small and you're right. They do go stale, don't they? I don't think any of us realized that at the beginning of our Internet marketing careers. You've got to keep putting new leads into your list.

Dan Norris: Yeah. Internet marketers focus a lot on the list, and I know the list is important. I can't be one of those guys who gets success doing something and tell people that it's actually no good, because I did rely on my list a lot. At the same time, I built a brand and a general audience, and a lot of the people who know about what I do aren't necessarily on my email list. It's not because I'm really good at social media or anything else. It's just, I think, because ... I don't know why it is. I think my content is so freely accessible that I'm not aggressive with getting people onto my email lists at all. I don't have popups or anything like that.

I give away a lot of free stuff. On my site with that opt in, I'll put up our recruitment guide on exactly how we recruit people. It's about 6,000 words and it's just a normal blog post in our site. A lot of my stuff is just freely available, and I think a lot of the people who are aware of what I'm doing just go to the site occasionally or see a post I put on Facebook or something and it's kind of a small loyal following, as opposed to a big, direct relationship.

Nicola: Content marketing, in giving value, like you say, without being aggressive about forcing people to get on your list to read the rest of it, it [causes 00:55:23] an awful lot of goodwill. Then when you go and ask people to help with something, they're much more likely to do it.

Dan Norris: Yeah, that's right, and that's one of the things I noticed in Pat Flynn's audience. Just about every person who asked me to review their site, the first thing that happens when I go to that site, I'm perusing the site trying to work out what this website is all about, and I get hit with this popup that disturbs me and stops me from reading their content and makes me feel like I don't like them. Doesn't give me any value at all, just tells me to get on their email list before I even know what they do. That's never been something that I've really been that keen on. I want people to read my content. I want them to understand what it's all about. If they want to sign up, then that's cool, and I have ways of encouraging people to sign up to the email list, but I think you need to be a little bit more in favor of creating value for people than you are in taking from them. That's certainly something that's worked for me.

Nicola: Which is also a really nice way to do business, isn't it?

Dan Norris: Yeah, and it's just come from what I want to do. It's actually lucky for me now, because for quite a while ... It's easy to say I live doing content this way, but when it's not really working that well in terms of business, you don't have that much credibility. Now that business is going quite well, I can do whatever the hell I want. If I want to create a book and give it away for free, then if people don't like that, then that's cool. If it's not the latest IM technique then that's cool, but I've got the luxury to be able to do that now.

Nicola: Yeah. Does WP Curve use anything like ... Also you do content marketing, you got a list. You've got ambassadors, and you're obviously pretty active on certain social media. Do you do anything like Paper Click?

Dan Norris: No, we don't do anything. The only thing we do that is any form of marketing, really, other than content, because we put content on the side and I do lots of podcast interviews like this. Alex does a writing column for Forbes and he presents at conferences and networks and that kind of stuff. In terms of paid content, the only thing we do is we have a tiny ad roll budget which just shows people ads if they've been to our site before, like a retargeting thing. It's $50 a month. I just turned it on the experiment with it, and then I couldn't be bothered turning it off because occasionally some people post them on Facebook and say, "Well, you guys are really smart. You've got these ads." I'm like, "Oh yes, that's good." I'm not good at paid ads. I didn't really want to do them. I just preferred it. Plus, we're growing way too fast as it is, so we don't really want any more [crosstalk 00:57:57].

Nicola: Yeah, absolutely. You're trying to keep up as it is, so more customers. That's so interesting that content marketing's working so well for you and appearing on podcasts and things. Tell me about your business money. Have you always been good with money? Have you always been terrible with money? What have you had to learn about money and running a business and all that stuff?

Dan Norris: I've always been terrible with money and I'm still terrible with money. I don't know how to answer this question. The only thing I would say in terms of business, which makes it infinitely easier, is to build a predictable revenue business, and in our case recurring revenue is the best option if you can do it. You can't always do it, but that just makes absolutely everything easier, because you can plan everything. You can hire before you need to, because you know that revenue's going to grow next month. I was hopeless with the inconsistencies of running an agency, but the predictable revenue business is just a totally different animal.

That's probably the number one tip. The number two tip is that I have a spreadsheet that I actually included in the book. It's free on our site. It estimates our revenue and our expenses live at any given time, and we still manually update that every day. The reason I do that is because no matter how up to date your accounts are, it doesn't really give you a clear picture of what your upcoming expenses are or what your upcoming revenue is. Not on a rolling month basis. If you're growing 15% a month, it's a huge difference if we look at our finances on the first of November and the 12th of November, in this particular month, we've grown 10%. We've had 60 signups in 12 days.

Nicola: Whoa.

Dan Norris: Yeah, and we've employed three people. If I was to look at our accounting system, it'd be a totally different metric than looking at our little spreadsheet that just simply estimates what it looks like when we grow 10%, how many staff we need, what our expenses look like. We're continuing to use that spreadsheet. I've used it from day one, and I continue to use that. They're really the only two slightly organized things we do when it comes to money. As well as having a good accountant and a bookkeeper and keeping your books up to date.

Nicola: Yeah, you've got to have your back covered there. I'm a big fan of weekly cashflow forecasts that you update weekly at the very minimum. The fact that you update yours daily is even more inspiring because as a business founder, you have to have your finger on the pulse every single day, don't you? You can't wait for a month.

Dan Norris: Yeah. That's true. A lot of our assumptions and our decisions come from our revenue. For example, the amount it costs us to service customers comes directly from how many customers we've got, which directly translates in how many staff we need to manage those customers. Every X amount of customers sign up, we need to hire a new staff member. Every time we hire a new staff member, that increases our costs by a certain amount and we need to grow by a certain amount. Again, every time we would hire a new staff member, there's a direct cost for a whole bunch of systems that we pay per staff member. All of that kind of stuff. Literally if we're hiring once or twice a week or if we're signing up 10 or 15 customers a day, which at our absolute best we will do, then this kind of stuff, you really need to have a really good handle on this sort of stuff and an accounting system doesn't really give you that.

Nicola: No, it doesn't. Are you still largely a virtual company or do you have proper offices and grown up desks and things now?

Dan Norris: No. Both me and Alex work out of co-working spaces, so I'm in a co-working space in Varsity Lakes on the Gold Coast in Australia. He works out of We Work in San Francisco. We're up to, I think, 25 people now. That's including me and Alex, but other than me and Alex, they're all remote. Some of them work from home. Some of them work from coffee shops. Some of them work from co-working spaces. I don't think we're going to be anything more than remote unless we need to be. We want to employ someone in each of the three time zone as a project manager. It'll be someone like me or someone like Alex to replace ourselves. If, for whatever reason, it makes sense for those guys to work in our offices, we might do it that way, but other than that, we don't have any plans to open an office anywhere.

Nicola: That's brilliant too, isn't it, for anyone listening, because it means that you can grow an infinitely scalable company and keep it remote to suit your lifestyle, which is very cool.

Dan Norris: That remains to be seen. We've gotten as far as, I think, 650 customers, and I think we're up to 50 grand a month or something, but that's very far from infinitely scalable, so we'll see how far it takes us.

Nicola: What about your personal money? Do you invest in anything else apart from your business? Do you have time to even think about that? Or have you got any aspirations to invest in anything else in the future?

Dan Norris: I'm hopeless with my personal money. I've bought real estate before and lost money on it. I'm hopeless at saving. I'm trying to work all that out. I've got a bunch of different businesses, and so I think I might put a bit of money into my business. We'll probably buy some sort of real estate if we could figure out how. That's probably about it. I don't [inaudible 01:03:16] anything else I'm too excited about in terms of investing personal money.

Nicola: Yeah. Business is the way forward for you, then. Brilliant.

Dan Norris: It's the only thing that's really worked.

Nicola: It's the only thing that's really worked for you, yes. Tell me what you're most looking forward to in 2015. What's the next year got for Alex and Dan and WP Curve?

Dan Norris: Yeah, I've got WP Curve, which we just met for the first time last week and spent a week together in Hawaii, and I think probably a maximum of three hours for that week actually worked and planned out what we're doing for the next year. We've got probably 50, 60, maybe more, things, specific changes we're going to make that are going to be quite big. I'm excited about those. I've got my book, which is being translated into a bunch of languages ...

Nicola: Whoa!

Dan Norris: ... And continues to sell, which is really cool. I've got a startup called Helloify.com, which is a live chat meets team chat software application, and I'm working on that with my friend Luke who's in my co-working space. Then I've got another company called Black Ops Beer, which is a brewing company, which launched a week ago, where we're making craft beer. That could go somewhere really exciting next year as well, depending on what happens and if we can get some money and a few other things.

Nicola: I think I've seen some of the labels for that floating past. You were asking people's opinion at one point. It's very funky looking.

Dan Norris: Yeah, yes. I've been doing all the design for that myself and I'm not a designer, so I probably have been just putting them on Facebook and either saying, "Look, look, I did actually something that looks okay," or maybe asking people if they like it or maybe someone else [crosstalk 01:04:50]

Nicola: It looked very cool. It looked like the kind of thing that would be stocked in a Jamie Oliver restaurant.

Dan Norris: If you know Jamie, just let him know.

Nicola: I just interviewed Sarah Newton, who shares a book agent with him. Yeah, I'll keep my ears open for any opportunity.

Dan Norris: All right. Sounds good.

Nicola: Good stuff. All right, so that's just awesome, and thank you so much for spending an hour with me. I know that you must be incredibly busy at the moment and very much in demand, but I just wanted to touch base with you because your books had such tremendous impact on us and to thank you for that.

Dan Norris: That's awesome. I'm glad you read it, for starters, and I'm glad you interviewed me, and I hope it's useful to other people.

Nicola: Thank you very much. Dan Norris of WPCurve.com.

Dan Norris: Thank you. Talk to you soon.

4. RICH SCHEFREN

Nicola: Hi, it's Nicola Cairncross here, and it's the 100th episode of the podcast, and today I'm delighted to welcome a man who has made the biggest difference to not only my business life, but now the rest of my life, too, thanks to his groundbreaking transformation weekend I just attended in Delray Beach, Florida. Rich has completely changed the way I think about everything. He is an author, entrepreneur, internationally known business consultant, who's helped thousands of people build the online business of their dreams, including many household names online. A lifelong entrepreneur himself, Rich built his first $7 million business by the age of 23, and he first retired by the age of 25.

Bored only six months later, he got interested in hypnosis and decided to turn that interest into a business. Realizing his love was the startup stages of growth, Rich left the Hypnosis Center when it had grown to 13.5 million annually, and pursued his next passion, the Internet. Since then his Internet strategies have been taught to and used by Google, Microsoft, Yahoo, Agora Publishing, Motley Fool, thestreet.com, and Boardroom Publishing, not to mention Weiss Research Incorporated. Wanting to impact the world, he then founded his current business, Strategic Profits. His company's mission? To improve the lives of entrepreneurs worldwide by helping them to earn more while working less in their businesses. Welcome to the call, Rich.

Rich: Thanks, Nicola.

Nicola: What I'd really like ... Sorry, start again.

Rich: Just thanks for the introduction, too.

Nicola: You're very welcome. What I'd really like to do, Rich, is go right back to the beginning. Now, obviously I know your story inside out, but my listeners won't, so take us back and tell us how you became the entrepreneur you are today, and then we'll go into your best tips for business, mind, money, and marketing.

Rich: How far back do you want me to go?

Nicola: Well, you know, tell me about your family, where you grew up, and was there any entrepreneurial influences in your life in the early days?

Rich: Oh, yes, sure. I think I was blessed by that. My dad was an entrepreneur, kind of a ruthless entrepreneur, so I got to see the extremes of business, I'd say. I didn't want to grow up that way, but it was definitely a lesson, and he wasn't around very much, but because he wasn't around very much, I was always eager to be around him whenever I had the opportunity, and so a lot of that time that opened up for me, to be able to spend time with him, was on the weekends to kind of tag along with him on a Saturday when he would go to work or go to meetings, and I would join him.

Sometimes he would be meeting other business owners or doing deals, and I would just sit there and listen, and then on the way home he would describe like why he said what he said on the way there. He would kind of give me a perspective, and so it was always an educational experience for me. He treated me like an entrepreneur. I remember as a kid I used to wash his car for a dollar. I was like eight years old and one day he made the mistake of having me in the car when he took me to the car wash.

Nicola: Uh-oh.

Rich: When he took me to the car wash, I saw that he paid eight dollars for the car wash, and I was like, you know, a little bit offended that here he was paying the car wash eight dollars. I was only getting paid a dollar, and so I said, you know, "What gives here?" He's like, "Well, you know, that's what we agreed upon." I said, "Well, from now it's going to be eight dollars," and he said, "Well, if it's eight dollars, then I'm just going to take it to the car wash."

Nicola: Oh.

Rich: He's like, "You might want to charge me seven dollars so I have a reason to use you." That's the household I grew up in, and it taught me entrepreneurship, I guess, from an early age. Got involved in my own businesses when I was really young, and seeing the opportunity where other people didn't see the opportunity and I guess it's always come pretty natural to me, pretty easy. I recognize in my work with entrepreneurs for the last God knows how many years, that the way I see things is not usual, and so a lot of my work revolves around helping people see things the way I do see them, and I think a lot of the reason why I'm able to see things the way I do started all the way back then just being exposed at such an early age and that really being such a big part of my influence as a child.

Nicola: Yeah. It sounds awesome but terrifying. Didn't you go and do ... Didn't you try going down the normal sort of college and big firm kind of route at one point?

Rich: Yes. Yeah, I studied accounting in college, and I won a bunch of scholarships from Arthur Andersen and Andersen Consulting. I was top of my class in accounting. I took actually a year off and worked for them in my junior year, and I worked in every different division of both the Andersen Consulting and Arthur Andersen, and a very special kind of program where they're trying to recruit you, and they'll let you join any division, and so you take a year off and you try every division to see what resonates with you. It comes with a lot of training and it was a great experience, and I loved it, and I loved Arthur Andersen and

Andersen Consulting, now called Accenture. I was thinking that I might go down that route, and towards the end of my first semester of my senior year, in a conversation with my father, who owned a business ... He owned several businesses, but he owned this one business that was a store that was failing. It was losing a lot of money, and so he was going to close it.

It was never his passion, and it was just something that he owned and was useful at a time, and he was going to close it. Him and I made a deal that I'd drop out of school, not finish my last semester, and take it over. I would take it over, if I turned it around I would get 50% of the business and compensate him for the losses that he incurred from the point I took it over until it was successful. The lease was running out in a year and a half. That's when he was going to close it, and so I had about a year by the time I got there to turn it around, and if I did turn it around I'd get 50% ownership and he'd get reimbursed for all the losses. It was no-lose for him and no-lose for me, a win-win, and that's what I did.

When I got there, the business, the break even was about three million. It was doing about a million and a half, so it was losing about a million and a half, and we turned it around. It became a very well-known store in Manhattan. It was in New York City, and it went back to three million, then four and a half million, and then six million, then seven million, seven and a half million or so, and it was continuing to grow. We opened a music label. We put a recording studio in the store that turned into a music label, a techno music label where we had worldwide distribution on, and I recognized around that time that this was not really my lifelong pursuit, and so I gave the business back to my dad, went back to school, finished my last semester, and decided to take a year off and figure out what was going to be next for me, or kind of semi-retire. I kind of knew I was eventually going to do something, but not sure when I would figure out what or when, and that was kind of the first phase.

Nicola: The thing I was most fascinated about by the story of the store, not least because it grabbed my attention, because I was running a house and garage record label in London at the time, was your story about how you identified who were the best sellers, and really analyzed what they did and how many units people sold on average. The maths around that I found completely fascinating, and I think if you could just tell us a bit about what you did on the first day when you walked into that store. Did you observe for awhile and then start making changes, or had you decided that you knew what needed doing? Tell the listeners the kind of analysis you did to help people sell better in that store.

Rich: Well, you know, the first thing I did actually ... Well, I saw the store and the store was a mess. I mean, the clothes sucked. It looked a mess. Everything was bad about the store. What I then did was I actually flew to Europe and I flew to Paris and to London and then to LA to see what stores there were doing to get a sense of just what was hot.

Nicola: Yeah.

Rich: Then came back to New York and figured out a overall direction of what I thought we had to do. In the beginning it was not easy. We wanted to bring Diesel into the United States. They weren't in the United States at that time, and at first they declined. They didn't like the store, and I couldn't blame them. We ended up being the first store to bring Diesel into the United States, and we were supposed to be the first store to bring G-Star into the United States and then they decided not to come into the United States for a couple more years.

We really ultimately built a store and I keep saying we because I drafted my roommate in college to come with me, so we did it together. We built a store that we would love because we saw that no store was really catering to our demographic, and everything in retail is really about maximizing your sales per square foot. Everything that we did was really revolved around that. The way we got into the music business, and now it's pretty common for stores to sell music, but back then I don't think there were any clothing stores that sold music. We put a live DJ in the store, and I think ... I never saw a store have a live DJ before.

Nicola: No.

Rich: We sold the music that the live DJ was playing, and the rationale for me was that well, if we're going to maximize the sales per square foot of the floor space, why wouldn't we try to maximize the sales of the air space?

Nicola: Oh, so you were going up as well as sideways.

Rich: Yeah, so that's how we got into the music business. Then when that worked so well it was like, well why do we have to buy music from others? Why can't we make our own music and build a recording studio right here in the middle of the store? Then when it came to our inventory, the goal was, that we eventually got to ... It certainly wasn't that in the beginning. The goal was to turn the store five times a year, turn the inventory five times a year, which meant that we carried about a million and a half dollars worth of inventory, and turning it five times a year meant we sold about seven and a half million dollars. To turn the store five times a year, you have to sell about 10% of your inventory every week, because then it takes 10 weeks to sell through and there's 52 weeks in a year, so you would sell through five times in 50 weeks.

Nicola: Ooh.

Rich: With our buying, we looked at ... Every week we looked at everything that was on the floor, and anything that was selling more than 10%, we would want to know why, did we need to order more? Was that section of the floor space premium? Did it always sell better? So that we could learn more about which areas of the store sold better. Was there a certain type of display that made it sell better? We were always learning about that kind of stuff, and if it sold worse was it also because of the location? Eventually we learned where the dead parts of the store were, or was it bad and did we need to get rid of it sooner rather than later so that we could actually make room for stuff that sold better? We managed our inventory based on attempting to always have the right amount of stuff so that stuff sold at 10% through. If we're selling more than 10% through we wanted to have more of it, and if we were selling less than 10% through we wanted to have less it, which meant that we might need to move it or put it on sale.

Nicola: That's what the supermarkets do on a much grander scale isn't it?

Rich: I would imagine so. I don't know much about the supermarket business, but and then we managed our staff that way too. We had about 60 sales people. It's a big store, and they got paid commission 10 times ... They got 5% commission 10 years over their hourly rate, so the idea there is that in the retail business if you look at your sales as 100%, right? Sales equals 100%. That's your revenue. Then your cost of the clothing that you're selling is going to be some percent. Now we sold used clothing and new clothing, so we had bigger margins. Let's say on average our margins were about 70% when you combine new and used, so we had 30% of cost to goods, and so now we had left 70%. Our goal was to have the employees be 10% of sales as a cost. We incentivized our employees that they got commission, 5% commission, once they sold more than 10% of what they got paid.

Nicola: Yep.

Rich: If someone was getting paid commission, they were less than what we had budgeted and allocated for them to pay for themselves, and so they were on commission that way. Then at the end of every shift, every salesperson had to write down how much they sold in total, how many units per transaction, the average transaction size, and the ... Units per transaction, average transaction size, and I think average unit, if I'm remembering correctly. This was a long time ago.

We took the averages of the whole store on those numbers, and anyone that was below average, like someone who ... Let's say the average units per transaction was two. Let's say somebody was only selling 1.1 units per transaction, but there were some people that were selling three and four units per transaction.

Then we would have one of the people that was selling four units per transaction coach for the day someone who was only selling one unit per transaction, so everybody in the store ... Not everybody, but the top performers in each area were coaching fellow employees on how they did what they did. We were consistently getting better. Everybody was monitoring their numbers, and that just got the store better and better and better, and that's what we did with numbers. I mean, we looked at numbers in every which way we good, from inventory to sales people to air space. The other thing that I'd say that we did that was intelligent, outside of making the store a very unique experience from the DJs to the way to the store was lit, to the clothing, everything else, was that we sold people on the store.

In other words, our goal was to create customers. What we did that I think is very different than what most stores did and still do, is that whenever we got clothes from Europe, which a lot of the used clothing I got came from Europe, or even like when Diesel first came to the States and we brought them in, you know people didn't know anything about them, so we sold them on why the store was special and what we had done to find this brand. The used clothing that we got from Europe, because they were special pieces for the most part, like we had hang tags that said what made this item special [crosstalk 00:19:40]. Then when people came into the store, sales people were required to say hello and ask them had they ever been in the store before, as opposed to can I help you, because can I help you, people say no.

Nicola: Yeah.

Rich: The answer to the question, "Have you ever been in the store before," if they said no, then the employee was supposed to sell them on the store by telling them what made the store so unique, and that we have a recording studio in here, we make our own music. Everything that you hear was made in the store, that we have buyers all around the whole and every hang tag you'll see where this item of clothing came from and where the buyer found it, and the story behind it, and blah, blah, blah, blah, blah.

Nicola: Amazing.

Rich: If they had been there before, then they would tell them what was new, the idea being that if we sell people on the store first and then clothing second, we have a much higher likelihood of the person returning, and when they leave and somebody asks them what they're wearing, they can not only tell them about what they're wearing, but they can tell them about the store where they bought it, and it worked, and it worked incredibly well, and it was a great experience. It was a really fun time to be in my early 20s and have a multi-million dollar business, and especially have one of the hottest stores in Manhattan. We had a lot of celebrities that were clients.

Nicola: Yeah.

Rich: It was a really fun time. It just wasn't my passion in life.

Nicola: Yeah. I remember when I first heard you tell that story, I can't remember where it was, but I remember it made me very, very interested in the figures of any business from then on, and you repeated a similar kind of thing with the hypnosis stores, didn't you? You really analyzed your advertising and your statistics on how many people picked up the phone and called, how many people turned up, how many people went to book appointments. Again, another example of using maths to really analyze a business, which was amazing.

Rich: Yeah, and you know, I would say that that just ... My mother was a mach teacher, and accounting, that's what we do, so I was an accountant by training, even though I never went into accounting other than that year at Arthur Andersen and Andersen Consulting. The numbers don't lie, and it's the best way ... You always can find opportunity by looking at the numbers.

Nicola: Yeah. Now, I love that story and I've got other stories I'd love to ask you about, but obviously I've got you for a limited amount of time, and I definitely do want to get out of you your best tips for aspiring entrepreneurs. What else would you like people listening to know about your journey from then to where you are now? What do you think's important to tell people about what you've done?

Rich: Well, you know, as you said, I went into the hypnosis business and the hypnosis business for me was I saw an article about a hypnotist in Time Out New York. I'd never been hypnotized. It sounded interesting. I wanted to get hypnotized. I got hypnotized. I really enjoyed it, so I got hypnotized some more, found it fascinating.

Nicola: I'm amazed they could hypnotize you, to be honest.

Rich: Oh, yes, I'm highly hypnotizable.

Nicola: Oh, good.

Rich: It was a great experience, and I wanted to learn more, and as I learned more I wanted to do it, and then as I wanted to do it, I decided I would build a business around it. It grew and it became very successful, and it was another great experience, and it ran its course. 9/11 happened, which was a setback for that business and made me decide I didn't really want to stay in that business and stay in New York, but I learned direct response in that business, and I also learned how the mind worked and a lot of stuff that I took with me going forward, as I did in the retail business as well. Then I got online and I struggled quite a bit in the beginning, and eventually righted my course, so to speak, and then did pretty well online, then got into ... What's that?

Nicola: I'm just laughing because you know, the thought of you struggling in the first place is astonishing, but then didn't ... You got started with some sort of niche sites first, didn't you, before you came to doing what you're doing now?

Rich: Well, even before the niche sites, you know, I just bought into the whole biz op promise, and I kind of lost sight of what is true and what's reality, and it really wasted, I don't know, like a year and a half, two years of my life and really was somewhat tormenting to my soul. I mean, the amount I was struggling and the amount of self-doubt it caused in me, and so I was ... For people who are struggling now or who have struggled, I've been there and I know what that's like, and I know how much it sucks and how you start thinking that there's something wrong with you.

Nicola: Yeah.

Rich: That's one of the ... Just one, but it's a strong one, of the motivators behind why I do what I do, but what I would say that's ... When you ask me what is it that I want to share, is that when I look ... At each progressive point in my entrepreneurial career, nothing looked obvious to me about what the next step was for me, and there were times of struggle and there were times of confusion, and there have been ups and there have been downs. There were uncertainties and times when I just wasn't really sure which was the right path to take or what to do and whatnot. In hindsight ... You know, Steve Jobs talked about this.

In hindsight, all the dots connect and you got to have blind faith that all the dots will connect, and you have to have the wisdom every once in awhile to look backwards and kind of connect the dots of where you started to where you are now, and where's the trend there? Where's it pointing you towards? What's the lesson there for you to learn now in what decisions you need to make now? Where I think I've been blessed has been that I have been able to really mine the lessons of my past, one because I got into the habit of keeping a journal like 20 years ago, so I have this written record of every day almost, of the last 20 years.

I've been able to mine that to really not only connect the dots, so to speak, of the trend, but also to notice my patterns and to recognize what I needed to learn from certain experiences, only looking in hindsight, to stuff I was blind to at the time, and being able to then have an awareness of that going forward. I think that ... When I work with entrepreneurs, there's a lot that I can teach them. There's a lot of their blind spots that I can show them, but what will help them more than anything long-term is if they can really learn from their experience. Life is the best teacher, and experience is certainly the best teacher, and most people don't really tap into the learning that they could from their own experience, and as a entrepreneur, that's a tragedy.

Nicola: I remember when you first mentioned journaling, I didn't really do anything about it for about a year or so, and then I started on January the 18th, 2011, and I've journaled nearly every day ever since. I've filled five moleskin diaries, and it just makes a tremendous difference. It just helps you, like you say, become more aware of things, it helps you .. You have epiphanies while you're writing, don't you? I don't think it can be done on the computer. I think you've got to do it away from the computer.

Rich: Yeah, I don't know. I've never done it on the computer because I started before there were even laptops and stuff, and I enjoy doing it by hand. I also don't want any more records of what I write because I write my truth, and so I keep them in a safe and all that kind of stuff. Yeah, tons of times things come up while I'm writing that never occurred to me. For people who don't keep a journal, I think most people have had the experience of driving from point A to point B and not remembering anything about their drive.

They were kind of doing it on automatic, and I'd like to invite those people to consider the possibility that they're living their life that way, that they might not think that they're living their life that way, but I'm sure when they were driving they didn't think they were driving on automatic, but that they're living their life on automatic, and that by not stopping and kind of reflecting on a consistent basis, a year can go by, two years can go by, a decade can go by, and you wonder what it is that you really did. You wonder where that time went, why you're still close to where you started, and you have no concept that maybe you've been trying the same things over and over again just dressed up differently. For me, yes, the journal has been priceless.

Nicola: Yeah. We can't even begin to cover the story of the Internet Marketing Manifesto and your phenomenally successful BGS program, Business Growth System program, which is still going strong today, but I'm going to put lots of links underneath the podcast so that people can go and read your history and your achievements, but we seem to have segued nicely into your business mind, which I know is one of your favorite topics. What else would you like to say to the aspiring entrepreneur out there about how to think differently, how to think better?

Rich: Well, a couple of things, and then we kind of lead into what's most fascinating, I guess, to me right now. One thing is is that I was talking to ... This is just very relevant to me today because I was talking to an entrepreneur yesterday about this. I was talking to an entrepreneur who thought he had failed, and he thought he had failed because ... This was an offline entrepreneur ... Because he had a gym, a boxing gym, and he moved the gym and he was late on rent, and so he left the equipment there and the landlord reopened his gym. The landlord like stole a bunch of his clients when he opened someplace else, and he felt like a failure. The first thing I shared with him was that the same happened to Sam Walton, the man who would have been the richest man in the world if he didn't break up his wealth amongst his family. Sam Walton is the founder of ... Well, he was. He's dead, the founder of Walmart, Sam's Club, et cetera.

He opened a Ben Franklin store, a franchise, and the landlord didn't renew his lease, and then took over the franchise and gave it to his son, and Sam Walton was like never again. He's going to do his own story this time, because that wouldn't have been able to have happened. The same story happened to Sam and he didn't perceive it as a failure. He just perceived it as a setback, and then in my own experience, the times that I was most close to failure, I have had my biggest successes. Close to failure is a judgment call. It's subjective, but that this man that I was talking to yesterday, he hadn't failed. He lost 40% of his business, so he still had 60% of his clients, but he was seeing this as a failure, and I was telling him, "No, you're on your way to failing, and what you have to do is you have to have that be the catalyst for you to now get very determined, hungry, and light up in you every fiber of your determination to make it different."

That just is very relevant to me because that happened to me yesterday, and so for those entrepreneurs who are on the downside of things, just recognize that until you throw in the towel, it ain't over. You get to decide when it's over, and you can use where you are now to be the catalyst to make something great, and in fact, most people work the hardest when they're closest to failure, which is why they end up not being there. Something to think about. Where life has taken me recently is that we have two primary core programs at Strategic Profits. We have BGS, which you spoke about. It's the Business Growth System, which is really I launched back in 2006 when I wrote The Internet Business Manifesto. It's the program that pretty much most, if not all of the top Internet marketing gurus of today went through early in their career before they were known like they are known now, and has I think the best track record of any business coaching program out there.

That's been our flagship product for years, and that really teaches people the missing knowledge, like what people need to know that they don't know, and that they don't even know that they don't know about business. It's what I learned sitting next to my dad, and then sitting in Arthur Andersen and being exposed to all the different divisions and then all of the business experience I learned in the different businesses that I've grown and all of the business experience I had coaching and consulting to all these different businesses all wrapped up in one program. That's BGS. Then GPS was based on theory of constraints, which is a business improvement model which really, in my opinion, teaches people a very structured, formalized and powerful, extremely powerful, thinking process, because it's my belief that most people don't know how to think powerfully.

We created this program and applied it to entrepreneurial business basically so that we could teach entrepreneurs how to think powerfully, how to think in a totally different way, and it was as we expected, very effective and got incredible results as well. In those two programs ... We also have Founders Club, which is a monthly continuity where I share new insights, but BGS and GPS were the core programs and Founders Club is the way that we kind of stay in touch with our alumni as well as people who kind of first get introduced to us. In BGS and GPS, there's the knowledge and there's the thinking, but there was something missing and I really wasn't sure what that was. I mean, we get, I believe, better results than anyone else out there, but there were still people that weren't getting the outcome that I thought was possible for them. I recognized that they didn't really have a knowledge problem. They knew enough.

Some of them even thought well enough, but yet they still didn't get the outcome and it wasn't until I had a midlife crisis of sorts, where I kind of got to a point in my life where I had kind of had all the success that I had ever dreamed of and really started to reflect on my life, and felt somewhat dissatisfied, and kind of like is this all there is, and really went on a path of self-discovery that I kind of fell into a whole other area of study that was very relevant to where I was in the situation, but also very relevant to what was missing for what I now see for most entrepreneurs. That is is that who you wound up being, that we have these experiences in life that shape our beliefs about who we are and what we're capable of, and what's possible for us.

Most of these things kind of live underneath the surface for us. We're not even aware that we're unaware of them, but they limit the possibilities for us, what we see, what we don't see, what we think we can do, what we think we can't do, what thoughts we have, what thoughts we don't have, and so on. What I've come to recognize is that for most people the way they wound up being is not who they need to be to have the successful business they want to have and to be the successful entrepreneur they want to be, and to have the life that they want to have. That sets up a real problem, that how you wound up being is not who you need to be, and so I've created.

Nicola, you were at the very first time I've ever shared it, this entrepreneurial transformation program that shows the entrepreneur how they wound up being, like exposes it, peels back the layers of the onion so you see it for the first time ever, what's really been running your life, what has been going on that you didn't even know was controlling you so that you can come face to face with it and you can actually transform it, and transform it not just to anything, but transform it to who you need to be to have exactly what it is you want. It's a really powerful process. I studied God knows how much stuff for the last two years, using it all on myself first, recruiting ...

Nicola: Yeah, a test dummy.

Rich: Yeah, recruiting a doctor, a great doctor, to join me on this pursuit, and her and I are now bent on changing the world. Our goal with this is to really transform entrepreneurship basically from the inside out, to make it so that anyone can be the entrepreneur they want to be, and what's required is this kind of transformation process.

Nicola: Yeah. I mean, what I'd like to do now is just chuck out the rest of the agenda because having just come back from this weekend, I have achieved more in this last week, since I got back, then I have in the last three months before, and it was so interesting because I learned ... I trained as a coach back in '98 and '99. I did a lot of self-discovery. I've done therapy for years, and I think I thought of myself as a pretty confident person, but this weekend was the most unique experience I've ever had in my life.

There were astonishingly successful people in the room, but ... Obviously I'm not going to share anything about what happened but it was amazing that everybody had such similar issues presenting in different ways, from the most successful person in the room to the person who wasn't quite so successful. I listen to your dispatches as well, every single week as you know, and I've heard you exploring all these things and then applying them to your life. When did you decide that you wanted to put it all together and really take it out to the bigger world?

Rich: Oh, well, I decided that awhile ago, but you know, making the decision that I wanted to do it and feeling like I was capable of doing it, there was a big time lag between the two.

Nicola: Yeah.

Rich: What I guess I would also say, and this might be more for your benefit than even the people listening, but I have to say it only just to pat myself on the back a little bit, is that you have the benefit of being able to go through the process in a weekend. I did it, which means that when I surfaced like, how I wound up being and saw some of the ugly parts of myself, I was just left with that.

Nicola: Yeah, and they weren't helping you, supporting you.

Rich: Not for like two hours, but for weeks, and it wasn't pleasant, and it kind of sucked. That's what I mean by it was a real journey for me, but that's ... I've always used myself as kind of the guinea pig and I look at it like I'm smarter than the average entrepreneur, and I'm more flawed than the entrepreneur, so it's a gift, because I get to work out the problems for people, and then because I work out the problem I get paid handsomely for it and so it all works out well. Yeah, I decided once I started seeing some change in myself, I knew I wanted to offer something, but it probably was at least another year from that decision until I offered anything, and I could have delayed it even more, but I just felt that ... I was getting pressure from my office that they were seeing enough of a difference in me that like, "Look, you've got enough here. Look at you already."

It was that argument that kind of tipped me over, because when I thought about it that way, I was like, "Okay. It might not be complete from my perspective, but then nothing ever seems for me to be complete, but I know that the benefit and the difference that it can already make for people is so profound and there's nothing out there like this, that it would be a disservice to not release it." That's what kind of finally got me to put it together and now that we did, it's been massive planning and working on it every day since so that we really start to refine the process, make it stronger and everything else, and then you know, it's just so exciting.

Nicola: I can imagine. I mean, it was so interesting the fact that the letter that you wrote to your mailing list, the thing that brought us all into the room, all eight of us, was there was something different for each of us. We'd all read something different into the letter, but there was something that struck a chord with each of us about how we felt about ourselves, how we felt about our business, and what we felt was needing fixing. It was all very different for each person, wasn't it?

Rich: Yeah, and the ... I want to try and say this precisely. The ... There's a timeline for people that everybody for the ... Well, not everybody, almost everybody or a good portion of people eventually figure out that there's a disconnect between what it is they say they want and how they're making decisions and how they're really living their lives. Now some people ignore that disconnect forever. Most people don't, and the people that don't ignore that disconnect will often stay busy with attempts to try and "fix it" in ways that have not produced any kind of significant difference for any extended period of time, so if the person procrastinates they've read five different books on procrastination. They're still procrastinating and yet they're going to read a 6th and 7th book. They are avoiding the gap between what they say they want and how they perform by staying busy enough because they're working on it.

At some point, and it's different for each person, they ultimately, if they're honest with themselves, they recognize that the way this is all laid out is not going to work. It's only when you recognize that that your solution is not a solution, it's a distraction from what will ultimately get you what you really want, that you're open to really looking deeper than that. I say deeper, but I don't really mean deeper, because you know, it's kind of interesting. I was thinking about this this morning. With theory of constraints, when you look at a business there are ... You start with symptoms, and then you drill down into the root cause to figure out what are the core reasons, what are the fewest causes that are generating all these nasty effects, which we call the symptoms?

In your life it's kind of the opposite. You start with these problems, but you don't drill down. You drill up, if you can kind of imagine that, because all these problems operate inside a context that you create, like a way that your world is based on who you are, the way you wound up being versus who you need to be. I know that that can be heady for people who don't really understand these concepts, but I shared this on my ... Should I share that? I'm trying to think of what ... The best way to share it. I won't share that. I'll share something else. Procrastination might show up for you in lots of areas, but there are work areas where it doesn't show up. There is a context that you could create where the idea of procrastination doesn't even occur.

Instead of working on the problem, which shows up in a certain context, in a certain way of being. If you can kind of imagine, it shows up under a certain umbrella. What you need to do is you need to change the umbrella. You need to change what is covering you, and by what's covering you, that's like the space, the context, who you see yourself as and what you are related to. By doing that, the problems that you currently experience just disappear because they're a function of your current level of thinking and being.

It's kind of ... It's an overused quote, but it's the quote by Einstein about how your current level of thinking is the cause of the problems that you are experiencing and that the only way to transcend the current problems is a higher level of thinking, because inherent in your level of thinking currently are a certain set of problems. When you transcend your current level of thinking, those problems will disappear. Now, new problems can show up because that's just the way it is, but you eliminate the current problems by not getting rid of the problems, but by transcending them, by thinking differently, not thinking about the problems and trying to fix them.

Nicola: I've experienced that for myself totally.

Rich: There's a way of being in the world where your problems don't exist.

Nicola: Yeah.

Rich: They just, they don't matter.

Nicola: It was totally, totally amazing, and the first ... When I came home, the first sign I had that I am thinking and feeling ... Well, I felt completely different, but one of the first signs was that I wasn't afraid of the flight home and the landing. I normally wind myself up for a good 45 minutes before the plane lands, but I was so busy absorbing everything that I'd learned over the weekend and trying to work out the difference in me, I just didn't notice the plane landing. It was so fun. What are you most looking forward to over the next year? I've got an inkling, but tell everyone else what you're going to be working on and what's next for you?

Rich: Well, within the next year, Dr. Laurie Emery and I are going to take this to the four corners of the world. We started with eight people in a room in Delray, and I've done this before with BGS and GPS, but I've never had anything as powerful as this, as impactful as this, and as necessary as this, so in a year from now, this process is going to be all over the place, and it is my mission in life right now to share this with as many people as possible and to consistently and continually make it more powerful, and just ... My life right now is dedicated to this. This is what my life is about. It is so exciting. I mean, it's a cause that's not only bigger than me, it's a cause that has me bounce out of bed in the morning and excited to just move it along and get it one step further along.

I'm excited about each day because I know that a new possibility each day is opening up about what is possible with this work and where we can take it, and how we can really make a difference for entrepreneurs. Yeah, this is ... I'll be doing some other stuff in my business, as I always do, but this is my primary focus and it's really ... I was exploring this morning the idea that, and I probably will ... I'm not fully committed to it yet, because it just kind of depends on how Laurie and I roll it out, but I might ... I'm seriously contemplating running a report about this, a pre-report about this, and if I do, I will ... I'm certain it will download more than the manifesto, which has been downloaded at this point more than two million times.

Nicola: I just find that so ... When you talk about it it makes me feel so excited because one of the things I got out of the weekend was connecting to this podcast so totally now, because this is the 100th episode. It was something I knew I enjoyed, but I didn't realize how deeply I feel that it's my work now, and I got that directly out of that weekend with you, so it's very fitting that you're the guest on the 100th episode, and I really want to thank you for that. I just want to thank you for everything.

Rich: My pleasure. When you invite me back for the 200th episode, where is the podcast going to be?

Nicola: I know exactly where it's going to be, because I planned out the growth of the downloads based on the current download situation. It will be being downloaded more than 100,000 times. That would just be amazing.

Rich: That's very nice.

Nicola: Yeah. Thank you very much, Rich. It's an absolute joy to talk to you as always, and thank you very much for everything you've done for entrepreneurs everywhere, and I look forward to seeing you when you bring the transformation process to London.

Rich: It will be soon.

Nicola: Oh, good. Excellent. Thank you very much. See you soon.

Rich: Thank you. Bye-bye.

Nicola: Bye.

Visit Rich at StrategicProfits.com

5. Margaret Wright

Nicola: Hi, it's Nicola Cairncross here from NicolaCairncross.com, and today I'm joined by Margaret Wright who is chief Flip Chick at FlipChickCoaching.com. Margaret is a speaker, best-selling author, philanthropist, business owner, and one of the most sought after real estate investing consultants. By developing a simple and easy to understand system, laser focused on building generational wealth. She has helped countless individuals learn how they can divorce their day job and never have to live paycheck to paycheck again. She has been profiled and featured on The Wall Street Journal, ABC, NBC, and many more.

Margaret's passion is to help other people realize their full potential. She is the founder of Kyuki-Do Wasi, home for teen moms, and she started the home in Peru in early 2013. I hope we're going to hear all about that because I know you've just been down there, haven't you Margaret? So welcome to the call.

Margaret: Thank you.

Nicola: It's lovely to talk to you again. The last time I saw you, we were sitting on sunbeds in Grand Turk.

Margaret: That's true. That was a good time.

Nicola: We discovered rather weirdly, on those sunbeds, through me talking to your son, who is really one of the most delightful people I've met for a long time, that he plays Second Life and I play Second Life, and that through that we, my sister knows one of your best friends Jenni Host (also in this book!).

Margaret: I know, its a very small, small world.

Nicola: It's incredible, isn't it? I still reel with wonderment when I think about that. So I'm talking to your son, he mentions a name I recognize, who is a very successful blogger and internet marketer. I recognize the name because my sister was mentioning to it as being one of her friends in Second Life. Now my sister lives in a tiny town in England, I live in a tiny town in England. Who knows where your friend lives, but there we are meeting complete strangers in Grand Turk, the Cayman Islands. I mean I just find that so weird.

Margaret: It is, it is very, very peculiar and I love it.

Nicola: I know that you're very successful in your own life because you've just taken your kids to Chile, Peru sorry for an extended period of time, but what I'd like to do know is get to know how Margaret arrived at this point. Tell me all about yourself, starting at the very beginning.

Margaret: Well, I guess I could start the beginning with, when I was 18 years-old and I found myself pregnant, which I mean [crosstalk 00:03:36] maybe that's not the right way to say it, I clearly had an active role in that happening.

Nicola: That happening.

Margaret: It really, aside from the fact that obviously that's a big life changing event, in a lot of people, when they know my circumstances and they know that I was a teen mom, that they think, oh poor Margaret, it must've been so hard. I always saw it as a moment in my life where I was able to shift, and it's really served me very well. I was able to make a shift from it's all about me, to now I can focus on helping somebody else. For me it was just my tiny little baby, but I've really been able to take that principle and apply it to everything that I do.

What could've been the most devastating time in my life, I think, and it wasn't easy, by no means was it a piece of cake, I was waitressing in the morning and working full-time and going to school at night, so it was challenging, but it was all for a higher purpose and that was for my son, who you met, who was on the lounge chair.

Nicola: Oh yes, I stalk him on Facebook now.

Margaret: I do too.

Nicola: That's way too fun. [inaudible 00:04:52]

Margaret: Absolutely, absolutely.

Nicola: Well he's a very very interesting individual and he's a lovely person and he came across very differently to a lot of teens. He was very comfortable wasn't he, being around grown-ups, so you've done a great job with him.

Margaret: Absolutely. Yeah, he's brilliant, very focused, and I just look at where I was at his age and I'm so proud of him. I'm so, so proud.

Nicola: Well you've got to take some credit, a little pat on your back for you because you've obviously done a great job. So when you found yourself expecting like that, were your parents supportive, or did you really have to make your way on your own, or what happened?

Margaret: Yeah they were supportive, they were not happy. They were embarrassed. I think it was back then, as my little kids say, back then nobody would be proud to say that their 18 year-old was pregnant. They didn't want to tell their friends, yes but they did support me. I'll tell you the minute he was born, it shifted from you screwed up to, oh my gosh, the love of our life is here.

Nicola: Oh, that's amazing.

Margaret: I've actually been able to share that with several people who have been in the same situation. I volunteer at a pregnancy center here by my hometown, and I talk to these people, these girls, and I talk to their parents. Its not an ideal situation, but its life-changing and it can be, depending on how you look at it, it can be something that's just the most amazing experience.

Nicola: I think its a bit different in America as well isn't it, because you guys have somehow, all the young moms out there, go and work shifts and go to school still. Whereas here, it seems to be the minute they get pregnant they just give up.

Margaret: Yeah, yes.

Nicola: Very sad.

Margaret: I could see that.

Nicola: Okay so what happened then? You're working, you're going to school, which I think you mean college, and you're working and you're looking after your baby, so what happened next?

Margaret: One of the first things I did was go to the career center, and at the time I was going for, psychology was my major. I went to the career center, and I started by the highest paying jobs and ... the list said, it and something I didn't understand, it programming, it information technology, da, da, da, da, and I was like well, I don't know what it is, but it is what I need right now. I switched my major to computer science and information technology and computer science, but I'd never owned a computer, I'd never even tried a computer class and I switched and I started taking programming classes.

Nicola: Wow, and did you ... were you good at it?

Margaret: I cried every night in my first C++ class, and I did do it, and I actually got a transfer degree to DePaul and have my Bachelor's in computer science, it's crazy.

Nicola: That is incredible, I'm really impressed. I'm impressed by your focus. Thinking at that age, I need to find out what jobs pay the best money and that's it, and that's what I'm going to go for. That was a remarkable insight there I think.

Margaret: In a lot of ways it came out of fear. I was so afraid of what I would do, and I was pregnant. I was pregnant when I switched my degree, and I was so scared of, how could I pay for this baby, how could I live, how can I feed him, put a diaper on him, and so it became my strongest motivating factor.

Nicola: That's incredible. So you graduated and did well at that, and then did you go off and get a corporate job?

Margaret: I went off and got a mind-numbing corporate job.

Nicola: I can't imagine you in corporate life.

Margaret: Yes, yes. That was the big success right? You go to school, you get a good job and then you live and then you die.

Nicola: You live, you buy stuff, and then you die.

Margaret: Exactly. It didn't take me too, too long in that world to realize that having a corporate job, I was a complete slave, that they told me when I would show up to work, they told me when I could take a day off, they told me how I spent my day. It wasn't until I later was remarried and had my second child that I took maternity leave and, for the third time, I was working for a company that merged and I was let go. When that happened, my father-in-law convinced me against my wishes, to take part in the family business, which is a martial arts schools. Yeah, it was a huge shift, and for one year I made no income, and I can't say I ran it into the ground, but I certainly didn't grow it.

I went to the other extreme of working for myself, but not really having the mindset. I still had the corporate mindset of show up and they pay you, not add value and that's how you'll get paid. After a year I decided I was going to go back to the corporate job and in the meantime, when I started interviewing, my system that I worked in had a new version that I didn't know. It was the transition into .net, and I hadn't learned that in school so I thought, oh my gosh I have to start over.

Instead, I decided to learn how to run a business and in 90, no in 60, sorry scotch that, in six months I was able to take our school from 90 students to 300 students, and realize that I was really good at turning businesses around and taking something that needs improvement and making the improvements and creating a lot of value. Then I started opening up and selling martial arts schools, coaching, doing a lot of coaching to martial arts businesses, and we still have those businesses today.

Nicola: Wow, that is incredible. What made the difference? Well don't share anything with me that you're going to share in your tips in the tip section, of the interview, the mind, marketing and money. What do you think made such a huge difference between someone who didn't know how to run a business and was not very good at it, to someone who suddenly figured out how business works?

Margaret: Gosh, I'm afraid I might say something I might say later, but ...

Nicola: Okay all right, so okay, so how did you go about learning how businesses work? Did you start reading? Did you go to seminars? Did you get a mentor? What did you do?

Margaret: I did all of the above. I did, I started by questioning, is it possible to be successful in this business? I started looking are there other people, because I knew a lot of people who ran martial arts schools that had to work a full-time job and they would come there and work at night because they loved it.

Nicola: It was a passion, yes.

Margaret: Yeah. So I had to go out and find somebody who had that passion and they were also making an incredible living. I found those people and then I asked who their resources were, and I went to their resources and I studied them, and I implemented, and I studied, and I implemented. I was just, it was ignorance on fire, I was like I'll do it, if you tell me it works, I'll do it, I'll do it, I'll do it. We changed our entire business model, our pricing structure and what happened is it actually went down at first. Our 90 students went down to probably 70, because I pissed a lot of people off, because people were not comfortable with that change.

But then the new people who came in, the culture was so different and they loved to be there and they were happy to pay money, they would write me a check for $10,000 and say, thank you so much for everything that you're doing for my family, and I used to have to chase people down for $50.

Nicola: Yeah, so that's, okay, there's two takeaways here, one is the fact that you had the, again you had the clarity of vision to think, is there someone in this business making a success of it? I need to go and study what they're doing. Which again is not common thinking. The other thing is the bravery of the person who was running the business before, was that your father-in-law did you say?

Margaret: Yeah.

Nicola: Did you have to talk him into trying these changes, or did he, was he the kind of entrepreneur that was able to see that it was worth a shot?

Margaret: He was a great role model, and he will let you fall on your face, so I think he knew it could have gone either way. He was supportive and he's so funny, he would just shake his head and make this grunting noise, and oh I see. He's my Mr Miyagi.

Nicola: Yeah it sounds like it, he sounds like an amazing person. You turned the businesses around, you're coaching other business owners in the same sort of space, is that what your book was about? How did you start moving into real estate?

Margaret: I don't know if you or any of the listeners have ever worked with a spouse?

Nicola: I have yes.

Margaret: That has its own challenges, and especially the ... I'll just say that we go at different paces, and he grew up in the martial arts business, so it was his love, it was like his home, and I came in like a bull in a china shop to get the bottom line right, and so we butted heads a lot, I'll just put it that way, we butted heads a lot. For the sake of our marriage we decided that we should not be working together as closely. I transitioned to a role of consulting to him and the staff, and we still have several schools, and we also run an organization that has about 50 schools in it, that we provide support and testing and different events and such.

          I stepped out of the day to day, and then started to lose my mind, because I was used to working, and it wasn't working, like showing up and punching a clock, but just being in that energy and that creative mode and finding where you can improve things and fixing them. Because I had, I'd sold one of the martial arts schools and I had a chunk of money, and I decided I was going to go try real estate, because I saw a lot of people were making money in real estate.

          At that time unfortunately I didn't follow my typical MO, and I tried to do it on my own.

Nicola: Oh, no mentor, no training?

Margaret: No mentors, no training just a hot idea.

Nicola: Did you read any books or anything?

Margaret: I had not even read a book at that point. I had never read a book when I bought my first real estate property. I will say that I grew up, I feel like I grew up flipping houses, because my dad he was an electrician, and I say I flipped my first house when I was nine, because I lived in a house that we fixed up for the purpose of being able to sell it, but I would literally crawl out the window on the second floor, and I'd be scraping the paint off of the side of the house, and so it was really just child labor, but I was familiar with the idea enough to know that when my dad would buy and ugly house, and we would spend all of this time and energy in to fixing it up. Then we would get to live in a bigger house in the next house.

Nicola: It was still an ugly house that needed fixing up, the next one.

Margaret: It was still an ugly house, but it was a bigger ugly house.

Nicola: Yeah, my mum did exactly the same. We moved about nine times in 12 years or something, and the houses got bigger and uglier, and needed more fixing up every time, but it was quite ...

Margaret: We are kindred spirits, I thought I was the only one with that story, but now I know why we love each other.

Nicola: It's quit exciting as well. I think the other thing that moving frequently does for you, although you hate it at the time as a kid, it makes you very outgoing doesn't it? It makes you able to walk into a classroom full of new children and make friends very quickly.

Margaret: Absolutely.

Nicola: Yeah, cool. How did your first real estate deal go then with no back-up or training?

Margaret: Well my first real estate deal went like this, come in and you can put 5% down and it's pre-construction pricing, and so I got so excited that I bought three of them.

Nicola: Oh.

Margaret: Yeah, and I still own, I managed to only buy one of those, I got out of the other two contracts, but I still bought one and I bought it for 260,000 and now it's worth 85,000. I can't say I lost money on it because I keep it and the cash flows, but it was, it should have been enough to scare me away, but then, now here's where I got smart, so a little bit of pain and now I realized that, hey this didn't go so well, it's going down in price, not up, so let me figure out exactly what I did with the martial arts.

Who's done this? How did they learn how to do it? Then I was just consuming every piece of education and learning about all the different aspects of real estate. Then the second house I bought was a house I bought to flip, and pretty much we did everything right, and didn't make a ton of money on it, I think I was a little bit conservative with it, I think I made about 30,000 on it. Then I would take the money, I would buy another one, and then we just, we'd do this not very full-time, I would do about one a quarter.

It would be enough to keep me busy, kep me from getting into my husband's business too much, and losing our marriage, and I was also making some decent money, not a ton, and then after that I thought, the system I was following was missing the recurring income, so the passive income wasn't coming out, I was always having to flip the houses. I decided that my time was more valuable, like at this point now I've got three kids, so I wanted to spend more time with my kids, so I started to again investigate, learn about, and implement creating passive income, and so now that's the system that I teach, is flipping a house.

I call it the flip and flow formula, and it's flip a house, take all the profits and buy a rental property that will pay you indefinitely.

Nicola: Okay cool, so when are we talking now? Give me a year so I can orientate myself in the property market ups and downs.

Margaret: The house that we bought, that was the dog, I mean it's a beautiful high rise condo, was in 2005. Now when we started really ramping up was about 2008, 2009.

Nicola: Just as the old property market's starting to crash.

Margaret: Yeah.

Nicola: Does this mean you're talking better deals?

Margaret: I was getting phenomenal deals, and I was flipping them fast enough, I was flipping them faster than the market was crashing. It was not as good as my deals are now, because it's on the up-trend, but as long as I could flip then fast enough, I could still make $20,000, $30,000.

Nicola: Were you not dependent on the banks for mortgages at this stage?

Margaret: No, but I started with about $125,000.

Nicola: Okay, because you'd sold your business.

Margaret: Yeah.

Nicola: You were in quite a strong position compared to a lot of investors, because you didn't have to borrow money, so you could get good deals.

Margaret: Exactly yes, you would go in with cash. Sorry?

Nicola: Did you enjoy all this?

Margaret: Oh it was so fun, it is still so fun, it's just ... going shopping for, some people collect shoes, I collect houses.

Nicola: Yeah. You seem like a very creative person to me, so that's an enjoyable thing, because you can create deals and there's nothing more exciting than creating money out of thin air, is there?

Margaret: Absolutely, absolutely, and to go into a house, I would go in sometimes with the realtor, and they would say, oh we shouldn't even go in to this one, and cover your mouth, there's mold in it, and I would walk in, and I would take a big whiff and I would say, oh it smells like money to me.

Nicola: I remember when I walked into my hotel for the first time, there was, which I did no money down, having read Russ Whitney's book, Rags to Riches Through Real Estate, and ...

Margaret: Oh, I was with Russ last week.

Nicola: Oh were you, oh my goodness, well I read his book one morning, it was Sunday morning in the bath, and I got up and I though, I wonder if you could do that in the UK? What I've been doing is I've been finding lots of little deals, I went and found a great big deal in a half million pound hotel. I remember when I walked in, the dining room, they'd given up on the bed and breakfast, and they had the place full of Thai nurses who were working at the local hospital, and they'd all been stir frying like crazy, and the dining room had a trail of grease across the dining room.

I think there was a shag pile brown carpet in the dining room, and it had been walked across by people who had been standing in the kitchen, they'd been stir frying. It had a trail of grease across it, and I just walked in and thought, this is lovely.

Margaret: Smells like money.

Nicola: It put everybody else off, Russ told me.

Margaret: Yeah.

Nicola: That's great.

Margaret: That's brilliant, perfect.

Nicola: Okay, so your real estate career is going great guns, and how, where does the book come in?

Margaret: The real estate, I was slow and steady, slow and steady, and I think I got bored again, and decided that I wanted to, not just do something that was the same, and granted every house is different and it is always fun and exciting to me, but I needed more. I needed to figure out something more, and I found myself talking to people and teaching people what I was doing, but in some ways because they didn't have all of the education that I had, I think maybe I was doing them a disservice because I was teaching them what I was doing, but not all of the details of it.

     I realized that I needed to create a system. If I can do it that's fine, but if only I can do it then what value is there really in that? If I could create a system where anybody could plug in, follow from steps A to Z, and at the end of the day be creating passive income. I started writing out what I was doing as I was teaching people, so that turned in to a book format, and also projects and webinars and ... I think it really, and the drive behind that, I think that too, when I found myself pregnant, was it's not about me any more.

     You can only do the same thing for so long, and if you're not helping other people and sharing with other people, for me I get bored, I don't feel fulfilled, if its me, me, me, me.

Nicola: Have you ever done the Roger Hamilton, Wealth Dynamics Test?

Margaret: I have not.

Nicola: Oh, well look it up after the call, because if you ...

Margaret: I will.

Nicola: Roger Hamilton, Wealth Dynamics. I'd be so interested to know what profile you come out at. You're obviously a raging creator, but there's probably a little bit of something else in there as well. It's very interesting because it tells you how to position what you do to be in the flow, and it sounds like you need to be creating and sharing. People often wonder don't they, why people teach what they've learnt when, instead of just getting on and doing it themselves? It's so much more rewarding to share though isn't it?

Margaret: Oh it is, that's 100% true.

Nicola: Is that how you ...

Margaret: I'll do it right after the call.

Nicola: Yeah, right after the call, so is that how you ended up being featured in all those magazines and things, because you ... and newspapers, because you wrote the book?

Margaret: Yeah, I've been interviewed a few times, and the interviews ... When I talk to people, and I explain to them what I do, to me it seems so simple and so systematic, but as I talk to people I don't ... I feel like I've just ended up in the right place at the right time, and just last week I was talking to a writer for Forbes, and he said, oh I want to do an interview, I want to do an interview with you. Again I think if you're coming from a place of giving and from your heart, that people want other people to know about that.

Nicola: Yeah, they want to share don't they? If they feel that someone's genuinely wanting to share themselves, they'll help you and want to share as well. Your kids, I should say your children aren't that old still, are you, so all this must have happened in the last few years.

Margaret: Yeah, I have, my oldest one that you met, Tyler, he's actually interning right now in Florida with Dave Vanhoose, and ...

Nicola: Oh is that where he's working, I wondered where he was with the swimming pool [inaudible 00:25:55]

Margaret: That's where he's working yes. Then my two little ones, one just turned eight on Monday, and then that's Braden my daughter, and then Nathan is going to be 10 in about a month, and now I home school them, and so that's been so much fun and I may be getting into one of the things I'm going to share, but it's another area where I realized that I want to make sure that I'm doing my best and hiring out the rest. I've have a tutor now come in a few hours a day to help with that.

Nicola: You've just been ... Before we move into the tips section of the call, tell me all about your trip to Peru?

Margaret: Oh my trip to Peru. That was part of my home schooling experience, and I'm a big fan of experiential learning. It's one thing to talk about the pyramids, but when you're sitting at the bottom of the pyramids it's an entirely different experience. Like you can't describe pizza, you have to take a bite of it in order to really understand it. It started as, we've got a Spanish tutor on Skype, and maybe we'll go visit him, and if we're going to go visit, then we should go see Machu Picchu and a long story shot, we ended up spending a little over two months in Peru, for the purpose of learning Spanish and understanding the culture and learning about South America.

In the process ... And we also were going to volunteer at an orphanage, and when we walked in, the first day I walked in, I just, I had such an overwhelming sense of responsibility and I can make a difference, that within a month we had opened up our own orphanage specifically for the teen moms, and of course that's close to my heart, that were living in this orphanage with no education, they were allowed two diapers per day for their babies, there was no food, they would bring, they would have food volunteers, people would volunteer and bring food in, but it was leftover food.

They would have to sort through the rotting piles of food to try to find enough to feed themselves. It was awful, absolutely awful. Now my focus shifted, I stopped taking my Spanish classes, so unfortunately I'm not as fluent as I had intended to be, but I stopped going to classes, and I put all of my energy into what do we need to do? How can we find a place for these girls? How can we find the, even find the girls? Just where are these girls?

We had them at our orphanage we were working at, there was three girls in particular that were teen moms, and they were teen moms, not like we are teen moms in our first world country, they're teen moms because somebody raped them. They're teen moms because their mom's boyfriend, being molested. Yeah, and they became moms at 13 and 14.

Nicola: Oh that's awful.

Margaret: Yeah, it was so hard, but it was also beautiful, because you would see these little mommas that just loved their babies to pieces, and they don't have anything but the love. To see that that's really what matters, and if that's the foundation, and you give them some resources, you teach them, you give them an education, then I just feel like they could do anything. It doesn't matter what their circumstances are or where they came from, if we support them and we give them a chance, and what an amazing, amazing feeling.

Nicola: In the same way that you were able to go to school and work different jobs, but they just don't have any of that, those options.

Margaret: Yeah, they don't have the support system. They could go to school, but nobody's going to watch their baby. We opened a home specifically for teen moms, so the girls come, we have a day care provider there so they can go to school, they can come home and they can do their homework. It's not just, you need to cook and clean because you're the oldest out of all the orphans. We are supporting them in a family environment just the same way we would our own kids.

Nicola: That's amazing, and that was last year you started that?

Margaret: This year, just in January we went down there.

Nicola: Oh I noticed, you must have gone straight after the cruise.

Margaret: Yeah.

Nicola: That's amazing. Again I was talking on Facebook, so ... And so what made you decide to home school your children?

Margaret: I wanted to travel. It was totally selfish.

Nicola: Yeah absolutely, I've been talking to Tracy Repchuk and Dave Repchuk on this podcast as well, and they're an amazing, well we saw them all in, again on the ship didn't we? They said, that was it, their kids got to senior school stage and the realized that they weren't going to be able to carry on traveling as a family unit, and that's what they'd been really enjoying doing, because the schools were getting so difficult about it, so they decided to home school them, and they've been traveling ever since,

Margaret: Yeah, and there's so much to be taught outside of the traditional school system. That's pretty easy to teach, you can teach the reading, writing and arithmetic in a couple of hours a day, so our schedule, we have four hours of school per day with the tutor, and then we spend a lot of time, my kids watch TED Talks every day, we have a field trip very Friday. They don't know ... When my kids were in school they didn't want to come home and spend time learning things that I knew they weren't going to be learning in school.

It's amazing how now they, the tutor actually, she just came in, right before we started he call, and she was talking about how she's just shocked, because she's a teacher, she's a regular teacher, and she said she cannot believe how much they're learning and how fast they're learning. She said she just loves the environment that we have with this home schooling with the tutor, and then we can also take them anywhere, anywhere any time, and they connect. It's amazing too, like my daughter's birthday was on Monday, so we took a bunch of her girlfriends to a resort, a water park resort, and you get things for a fraction of the price when you're flexible with your time.

Nicola: You don't have to go when everyone else is there. [inaudible 00:32:11]

Margaret: Yeah and I don't have to wait in lines at the water park, it's beautiful.

Nicola: It's quite interesting, because I've always well I was a complete dunce at school, and I'm so quick at learning things now because I want to, and I was always so bored because everyone else was so slow, it was painful.

Margaret: It is.

Nicola: Yeah, and my kids, like I knew they had to go, never knew I'd never have the patience to home school them, but I didn't know you could do it on he internet, and so they've been through the whole school system, and luckily for me they've elected not to go to university, they're both doing vocational studies. I'm just waiting until they come out of that whole system so that I can get my hands on them and ... But I've been teaching them about real estate and all that stuff, and how it's not about a well-paid job, about getting, working, making yourself free. It's the difference between what you spend and what you learn and what you invest in.

Margaret: Yeah.

Nicola: Great stuff.

Margaret: I'm trying to convince my oldest one to drop out of school and he will have no part of it, but he is learning both the wealth creation and ... He says he goes just for social reasons.

Nicola: Yeah, when I met him he was telling me he had a job in a coffee shop, and he loved it, but he never spent any of the money, he was just going for the social life.

Margaret: Yeah, he's like, it just gets deposited into my account, I don't need it, I just love going there. Very cute.

Nicola: Yeah, that really struck me, and the other thing that struck me was how he was like a sponge, he was, as I said, he genuinely seemed to enjoy the company of older people, which is quite unusual for his age, but he had so much to contribute to the conversations as well, but he was like a sponge as well, he was just listening to everything and taking it all in. It was quite incredible to watch.

Margaret: Yeah, oh, that makes me happy.

Nicola: Well I guess it does, doesn't it? Okay, let's move on to the tips but now, and let's find out from you what you would like to share if you were talking to a new or aspiring entrepreneur, either online or in real estate or in business indeed. What's one of the things that, the most important things around your business mind that you think a new entrepreneur needs to know?

Margaret: When I think about the business mind, it's not something that is just automatic, so for me I am very deliberate about my thoughts, so I will really, really guard the information that gets put into my head, and the information or the thoughts that come out of my head. I love to do incantations or do self talk. A couple of them, I was running with my husband this morning, and we just started shouting them out, I'm sure people think we're crazy. I'll say, I'm a lean, mean sexy machine, or I'm clear, I'm here, I'm kicking into gear. They're silly things, but having that thought of I can do this, I can take any idea that I have and turn it into reality.

As opposed to a lot of people, they, again I guard against people who are going to have negative thoughts towards me. If somebody comes to me and they're like, oh this isn't going to work, I will do my best to coax them into a different mindset, but unfortunately as an entrepreneur you have to be really selective about who you let into your life, because they will affect the way you're living, they will affect the results that you're getting and the way you see things.

Doing the self talk I would say is a huge one for me, and then guarding who you're spending time with, your peer group is huge.

Nicola: You're obviously a great believer in training, mentoring and I know you're in a mastermind group with some amazing people as well aren't you?

Margaret: Yep, and it's not something that just happens, by chance. I think you have to be deliberate about it, you have to seek out the people that you want to be inspired by. There's the two sides to it, I see that there's a part of, we want to be able to contribute, and there's always going to be people that you are feeding, and I think that we have to be deliberate about who we're being fed by, and know which is which.

Nicola: Yeah, that's really interesting, and do you feel that people need to have a bigger reason why than just them and their own success?

Margaret: Absolutely. Absolutely, and it's funny, our bigger reasons outside of us really are still about us. When I think about the orphanage, of course I did it because I want to help these girls, but it's the feeling that we get when we're helping somebody else, and if somebody's not really gotten outside of themselves and been able to help somebody that way, they're missing out on the most rewarding, the biggest high in the world is somebody else really, really appreciating something that you've done for them or been grateful or just to see somebody else's life turned around because of something you've done. That's amazing, that's an amazing feeling.

Nicola: Yeah, one of the things I most want to do is to invest in other businesses in terms of being an angel kind of person. Either investing skills or investing money one day, but in the meantime I used Kiva as a way of doing that, so every time I feel a little bit wobbly, I'll go and put some money into my account in Kiva, If you don't know about Kiva, kiva.org is great fun, it's where you can invest in micro-businesses around the world.

Margaret: Oh yes.

Nicola: You make loans to them through the Kiva Organization, and the Kiva Organization makes sure the money gets used for what it's supposed to. Then the entrepreneur, who can be anywhere in the world, and you can specify whether you want to invest in males, females, what kind of industry you want to invest in, and all that business, and it's something like a minimum investment of $10, or I think it goes up to $50 is the maximum loan. It's loans really, not investments, so you don't end up having part of their business.

They do pay it back, and then you get the money to play with again, so it's just really good fun, and you feel really empowered that you're empowering other people as well. It's not hand outs, it's something that's really actually helping someone build a business on the other side of the world. I find it really exciting.

Margaret: That's amazing.

Nicola: Yeah. What about you marketing? If you were going to pass on some wisdom about the best way to market a business, what would it be? What's worked for you?

Margaret: I think the first thing is just to be yourself and be genuine, so if there's a difference between who you are in front of people and who you are sitting at your kitchen table with your friends, then that comes across to people. If you're the same person, no matter who you're in front of and who you're with, I think that as a marketing, just that authenticity as a marketing strategy is huge. Then another component of the marketing, and this isn't necessarily internet marketing, but it really goes back to the same thing we were talking about, if you think about what you can do for other people, then that energy, that synergy will always come back.

When you meet somebody new, for example let's say you're talking to a potential JV, if you first think of how you can help them in their business, and it may or may not be a good fit, but if you always are thinking about you can help somebody else, you will be perceived as a person who people want to do business with.

Nicola: Yeah, it's very interesting you say that, because I've just literally come of a recording with Pete Halm, who I know you've known for a couple of years, now he's the JV manager for Andy Shaw, and he was saying exactly the same thing, he always goes with the thought of, what can I do to help this person? Before he thinks about what he can get back.

Margaret: Yeah, so he does a lot of ...

Nicola: Go on sorry.

Margaret: I think there's a lot of gut feel too for good partnerships or good JV's, or even in all of the marketing if you can feel good about the person who's the end buyer, purchasing what you have, you know that you're adding more value than what you're asking in return, and always be genuine with that. If I'm going to sell a real estate product for a couple of thousand dollars, it's a no-brainer, because the person at then end, if they follow the system, they can make infinitely more money than that. To know that you're selling something, you have to have a product that's a valuable product for people, that they can really change their lives, whether it's by buying a physical product or information.

That if you know that your coming from a place of you genuinely want to help the person who is supporting you, they're the ones whose money is being filtered through your business.

Nicola: Yeah, they're exchanging their energy in the form of money in, you're exchanging your energy in the form of knowledge, and I you can give much more energy than the money they're passing over, then you can sleep at night, can't you?

Margaret: Absolutely, in a nice soft big bed somewhere in the Caribbean.

Nicola: There's been different things you've marketed over the years, from the martial arts schools through to real estate, now through to information products, have you found that the same kind of marketing methods work for all of them? Is there a recurring theme, or did you have to change the way you marketed each of the businesses as you changed and grew?

Margaret:　　Yeah, I've never thought of it, but I think it is the same, because when I'm marketing in the martial arts I think about who is the student that's going to be standing on the mat and what are they going to remember when they think of their martial arts experience? What are they going to tell their kids or their grandkids about when they got their black belt? What is that experience that they're going to have that I can provide.

　　　Then I look at the real estate and it's the same. I stand in the kitchen and I think, what is it going to be like for this family to sit here and have dinner? I really think about the end of, what the result is that they're going to have.

Nicola: Not just about the end user, but the experience the end user is going to have.

Margaret:　　Yeah absolutely, that feeling that they're going to have.

Nicola: The feeling that the end user's going to have. That's even better. That's brilliant. Then getting the word out about everything, do you find that just naturally because you're loving what you're doing your passion shines through and it opens doors, or do you have, I mean how are how marketing your existing website theflipchick.net which is know is quite a new website isn't it?

Margaret:　　It is, it is very new, it's actually still a little bit right now under construction, but that is something that, when I, like yes, I guess it comes down to the same thing, who is it that I am going to draw into the market and where do I find these people? If I was in the martial arts where am I going to find parents with kids? They hang out in a certain place, so online if I'm marketing to somebody on Facebook, a good demographic for example in the rel estate world, if I look at people who might have a chunk of money that they want to invest, and they want to get a better return than having it sitting in the bank, and they don't have the information to figure it out on their own.

I think of, who is my target audience, and who do they, where do hang out? If I have an idea that, if you're a recently divorced woman, you may have gotten a settlement through the court that you need to put somewhere. It will very easily leave you if you don't have the financial IQ to take care of it. Where would these people be hanging out? Maybe it's meet ups, maybe it's certain Facebook groups, maybe it's a church group. Looking at each of my avatars, and where are they going to be hanging out? Put myself I their shoes, if I just went through this, what would I be Googling, and all the information that they show up?

Nicola: Yeah, it can be even, that's ... I love the way that you've built a successful business around this, before you even had a website.

Margaret: Yeah, I know, it's crazy.

Nicola: It is, you're home online, it's like your shopfront online, but you've been busily running the business behind the shop for a long time haven't you?

Margaret: It really happened, I didn't wake up on day and say, hey I want to start doing real estate education. It happened very organically. I was doing what I was doing, because I loved it, and I knew it was a really great strategy for building long term wealth. Then people started to see our lifestyle, they would say, wait a minute, you've been in Peru for two months, and I know that between you and your husband you have 15 companies, how's it even possible?

I would just start talking about it, and it morphed into, hey this is a product that in order to serve the most people I need to box it up. I need to create it in a structure so that I can help more than just my friends and my family and people I meet on and airplane, to make it really, everybody deserves to have money, not just for them, but for their children and their grandchildren. [crosstalk 00:45:40] Sorry?

Nicola: Yeah, I'm not even going to talk about that generational wealth thing, you've obviously got your children firmly I mind there.

Margaret: Yeah, and really the timing of this too, I'm going to tell you a little side story, a few years ago my mom was diagnosed with a terminal illness, and she doesn't have any money saved up. She's got a little 401K, that's not going to last her for anything. I saw first hand, especially for a woman who doesn't have the resources to take care of herself, what happened? If it wasn't for me and my husband taking her into our house, she wouldn't be alive today, I absolutely believe that.

Nicola: Because the stress would have been so much for her.

Margaret: Yeah, she wouldn't know how she would have paid the bills, she wouldn't have, she couldn't even take care of herself, she was literally bedridden. How sad, that if you, if you don't have somebody there, I see it as a huge social responsibility to become wealthy. Because there are people that you can take care off, that will never be able to take care of themselves. Some of them you're going to educate so that they learn and they can do it on their own, and some people they become where we contribute, and where we have charity.

Nicola: I love those distinctions you're making there, because that's very true. A lot of people go to it, I've spent a lot of time in the wealth creation arena, having written The Money Gym, and a lot of people used to just really, they say, oh my mum needs this, or my sister needs this, or my brother in law needs this. It's like no, focus on doing it yourself first, and you can help everybody else.

Margaret: Absolutely. Empowerment first.

Nicola: Yeah, exactly. You said something else very interesting there, it's just nicked out of my head again. Oh no, I've got it, I've got it, it was when you said about boxing it up, it's people want to buy a definite product, don't they? They find it much easier to invest in a definite product rather than open ended coaching or consulting.

Margaret: That's true, that's true.

Nicola: That's what you've been working on, and I'll bet you anything you like when Tyler comes back from his internship with Dave Vanhoose, they'll be getting you on the stage as well.

Margaret: Absolutely.

Nicola: If it's not already planned for. Brilliant, so tell me about, that was all about marketing, but we talked a bit about money, but tell me what are the things you've learnt about money along the way, apart from the things you've already mentioned. Is there anything else you'd like to share with you a new aspiring entrepreneur?

Margaret: Well I grew up with a family that was very anti-wealth sentiment. My dad, it's the nasty, evil rich republicans, and we still, I mean we banter about it now, but that really was what I was taught growing up, that it's the rich people, not us, the rich people have money and they're selfish, and they got it by being shady and they're dishonest and I mean just every negative association to having wealth. Again I had to be deliberate about undoing a lot of that, about changing my perspective on what does it mean to have wealth, and again now my perspective is that it is something that I feel that I have to do to be able to help people in the way that I feel like it's my responsibility to help.

I can't do the things want to do. I couldn't open an orphanage without the financial resources. I could sit there and feel bad for these girls, or I could go out and do, and I couldn't make money in Peru, but I can come back home and I can kick butt with it, and I can make enough money to support that, so that they have an opportunity. Now they're not going to learn what I teach, because that's not, it's not a strategy for a third world country, but I can use my resources to create something for them, we're actually opening you a bakery, that the girls are going to be able to work at and be able to sell bread, and then also learning English, because it's a huge tourist community.

If they learn English they will be in the top 10% of the people in the country.

Nicola: They'll be able to, if they've got a skill as well then they'll be able to go work in the hotels and all sorts of things.

Margaret: Yeah.

Nicola: You really had to unpick a lot of programming from your background then, did you, again did you get a mentor for this, or did you just work on catching yourself every time you had a thought that was less than helpful?

Margaret: I studied a lot under Tony Robbins. I would say he had the most impact on my belief system about money. That it's not gaining to get, it's gaining to give.

Nicola: There's nothing wrong with that, and the more you can help yourself the more you can help other people. I'll bet your kids are growing up with a very healthy attitude to money.

Margaret: Very healthy.

Nicola: Well Tyler, going to work and not even spending the money he's earning. That was great.

Margaret: I think it's interesting, I look at my husband, he grew up, he's from, well he was born in the Unites States, but his parents are from Korea, and they came with a very different financial blueprint. That you work had for your money, and you support the family and the business, so my husband had an interesting disconnect between working hard and making money. Tyler, he would go to work at the coffee shop because it was fun, my husband would help because it's the obligation to the family.

He had a similar undoing about, you don't do it just because you're doing the right thing, it is okay to work hard with the expectation of making a lot of money. It's not dirty, it's not wrong, because you can do so many good things with that.

Nicola: It sounds like you've been through an incredible metamorphosis from your early days, and you taken everybody else along with you, in a reality positive way. It's really a wonderful story.

Margaret: I'm so happy.

Nicola: Yeah, I can tell, I can tell, you always sound like you're smiling, and I know there's ups and downs in everyone's life, but you've just got an energy that just shines off you, it's really quite amazing.

Margaret: Thank you.

Nicola: Your very welcome, so what's next for 2014, what are you looking forward to in the next year?

Margaret: This year, in 2014 I'm really ramping up the real estate education and creating products that people, wherever they're at, if they're an investor, and I call an investor somebody who has money, not somebody who's looking for no money down, that are an investor who's got money, they're going to have a strategy, and I also, because I very much came from unique meager beginnings, that it doesn't mean you have to have a huge chunk of money. There are strategies that you can follow, for example partnering with somebody who has money.

Really covering the bases for somebody who ... First and foremost, if somebody has the mindset that they want to build wealth, and build generational wealth, and anybody who knows anything about wealth knows that either, the people who are wealthy either built it through real estate, or are currently investing it in real estate. It is going to be a component to wealth, and having that generational wealth in your family. I want to be able to educate people as to first believing that they deserve that, believing that it is important for people.

There's no shame in saying that you want to be wealthy. Like there's no, there's really nothing great about being a money miser, and thinking scarcity. First shifting the mindset from scarcity to abundance, and then giving tools to people, so that they can, whatever pace is going to be right for them, and I'm not delusional to think that my way is the only way, but the education so people understand that hey take what works, take what else works from somebody else, but build your generational wealth so that you can make a difference for people.

Nicola: Is sounds like my family. Yeah brilliant, and I think the other thing is when people look and talk, look at you and talk to you, they ... You're very accessible, and I think they will think well, if she can do it I can do it, because you don't come across as a really high powered business person, although you have been. You come across as a very accessible and warm down to earth kind of person. The other thing is, you've actually done it yourself, so you really are coming from a place of authenticity, and I think that's another thing that people can really smell a mile off isn't it?

Margaret: That's true, that's true. I'm teaching what I've done, and I know that there's a lot of other thing I could be teaching, there's a lot of other ways I could make money, but to be authentic and be genuine, and any question they ask me I can answer from first hand experience.

Nicola: Yeah, and you've done enough of it, you've had the ups and the downs as well, so you can really identify with that can't you? There's [inaudible 00:54:33] beliefs a mile off as well can't you?

Margaret: Yeah.

Nicola: Good. Well Margaret it's been absolutely brilliant. I knew I'd enjoy this hour enormously, having spent some time with you on the ship and everything, and people can find you at theflipchick.net

Margaret: Yeah, or Facebook /theflipchick, you can follow my flips that I'm working on and all the antics of being in that business.

Nicola: Yeah, that's fantastic, and we'll also put loads of links underneath the podcast, so, well thank you very much, we've had a lovely time and it's come to a close all to soon, but ...

Margaret: Thank you so much Nicola, I loved it.

Nicola: I look forward to seeing you again very soon.

Margaret: Okay, cheers.

Nicola: Okay, bye Margaret.

Visit Margaret at FlipChicksCoaching.com

6. RYAN LEVESQUE

Nicola: Hi, It's Nicola Cairncross here with another episode of the podcast. Today, I'm delighted to be joined by Ryan Levesque, creator of The ASK Method and author of the bestseller "ASK!"

In 2008, armed with nothing but a 450 dollar laptop, an Ivy league background in neuroscience and an insatiable curiosity to understand why people buy, Ryan left a lucrative career on Wall Street and later in Shanghai, China, to launch a multimillion dollar online publishing business selling information and software using what's now become the ask formula as taught in his book. Ryan has used the ask formula to help build multimillion dollar businesses in seventeen different industries, generating over 100 million dollars worth of sales in the process.

Today, he and his team offer training, consulting and implementation services for entrepreneurs and businesses at all levels. Ryan, I'm really delighted to welcome you to the call today, because I am a customer of yours, as you probably know.

Ryan: Nicola, I am so thrilled to be here. I just wanted to say thank you so much for the opportunity to be here.

Nicola: Really looking forward to hearing all of your story, so start from the very beginning. Tell us where you were born, what your family was like, and how you became the entrepreneur you are today.

Ryan: Sure. I grew up in the northeast of the United States in New Hampshire. My family, I have French Canadian ancestry, my background is French Canadian, my grandparents are French Canadian from Quebec province, so hence the name Levesque and the crazy spelling. I grew up in a working class family. My dad was a shipping clerk. My mom cut hair for a living, and I was the first person in our family ever, extended family, ever to go to college. My parents were the first to graduate from high school. Both sets of grandparents left school at a very young age, and both my grandfathers were military veterans and entered into the military, fought in World War 2. For me to go to college was a really big deal. For me to go to an Ivy League school, which is in the States is very difficult to get into, as I'm sure you probably know, and very unusual for someone from my background to get there. Basically, pride of the extended family.

Things get a little bit worse from there. I go to school, and I thought I was going to become a doctor. I studied neuroscience. I thought I was going to be the next great neuroscientist, and that's what my family expected, so there was a lot of hopes and dreams put in there. Nicola, I realized when I was in university that I tell people there's smart, and then there's really smart. I was smart, but I wasn't really smart. I recognized this when I met someone who went on to be one of my best friends in life, a man by the name of now doctor, Dr. Charles Kassardjian. He and I were roommates, best friends through college, and he went to become a neurologist at the world-famous Mayo Clinic.

Nicola: Wow.

Ryan: Charles was really smart. I was just smart. I realized very quickly that I didn't have the chops, the-, I just wasn't smart enough to become a neurosurgeon. I just didn't have it. He did. I worked side by side with him, and I recognized that. You have to understand, so at some point in college, I had to come to terms with this. At the time, I was also studying something kind of random. I was really into Chinese studies, East Asian studies. Originally, I was really interested in the effect it had, East Asian-, excuse me, the effect that traditional Chinese medicine had on the brain. I was kind of studying Chinese with the intent of studying traditional Chinese medicine and the effect that it had on the brain and kind of tying science with that. I very quickly fell in love with Asian Studies and Chinese.

I had a conversation with my parents and said, hey, listen, I'm going to spend next summer-, this was my junior year of university, third year of university. I said, listen, instead of becoming a neuroscientist, I'm going to backpack through China.

Nicola: I'll bet they were thrilled!

Ryan: Loved it. They loved it! I said, don't worry, it's just temporary. I'm just going to, I really want to learn the language and just travel across Asia and just really expose myself to the culture. Eventually they kind of reluctantly said okay. My mom's first reaction is can you make money doing that? So anyway, went from neuroscientist to kind of this guy really interested in Asia. After university, didn't know what I was going to do, but I knew I needed to make some money.

As a kid, I was always interested in business and investing. People always ask, well, if you're this working class kid, how did you ever afford to pay for $40,000 a year at the time tuition. We didn't get any financial aid. It's a strange story, but the short answer is this: When I was ten years old, my grandparents passed away on my mom's side. They passed away 18 months apart. After they passed away, they left me a $5,000 inheritance. That was everything that they owned. That was all that was left after funeral costs, and we didn't make any money selling their house. It was five thousand dollars to me in the will. My mom said, you can do whatever you want with this. Sorry, I'm getting emotional.

Know that this is their legacy to you. For whatever reason, a ten year old really interested in investing. At ten years old, this is at the start of the early 90's, late 80's, early 90's for me, so the stock market is really taking off. My mom had this book, it was called the Beardstown Ladies Guide to Investing. It was this investment group of these old women that created this investment-

Nicola: Oh! I know about this. I know about this, because I got very interested in investing when my ex-husband was left a load of shares by one of his aunts. That's why I was resonating with your story there. We found out that-, I went on a mission. I was pregnant with my second baby, and I went on a mission to find out all about it, and I heard about the Beardstown Ladies. They're very well known in the investment world, aren't they?

Ryan: Yes! Yes. They made all this money, I think it was mostly in the 80's, and I think one of my mom's friends lent her the book. It was on our coffee table. I read the book cover to cover. Crazy, right, as a ten year old. I was hooked. I went to the library, got every Peter Lynch book on the market, Learn to Earn, One Up On Wall Street, all of those books, and became obsessed. I said, well, Mom, here's what

I want to do. I want to take that $5,000, and I want to invest it in the stock market.

This can be my, that's going to be Grandma and Grandpa's legacy. Long story short, by the time I turned 18, through a lot of luck, but some smart decisions, grew that to $85,000.

That paid for my first two years at Brown, and then on top of that, all through high school, basically as soon as I could work at age 14, worked three jobs. I was a janitor at our local school system. Buddy of mine got us in. It was actually a pretty decent paying job, as unglamorous as it sounds. We got paid $10 an hour, which at the time was like really good money.

We were-, I was a cashier at the local grocery store, at Shop and Save, which we affectionately called Shop and Slave, because they treated us like slaves. Then I had a landscaping business with the same buddy that was a janitor with me. What we would do is the janitor job in summer, like between the summers in high school would start at like six in the morning. So we'd get to school really early, we'd wrap up, we'd work like 6 to 3, 6 to 4, something like that, a shift like that, and then at 4:00, we'd immediately leave, and we'd run our landscaping business.

We were cutting lawns, putting down mulch, doing trim, that sort of thing, and we'd work until dark, which was basically in the summer about 8:00 at night. We had like four hours to work at night. We did that Monday through Friday, and then on the weekends, I'd work ten hour shifts at Shop and Save. Between saving all that money and the investment money, put it all away, and invested in education. When I came out of school, I was broke. I didn't have anything, right? I needed to make money.

Nicola: But no debt. You came out of school with no debt, whereas most people come out with so much debt, don't they?

Ryan: No debt. That is something I'm so grateful for to my parents, to my grandparents for putting me in that situation. Because you're right, so many people graduate from school, and they're in a ton of debt, and it's a shackle that holds them back. It's so fortunate that I wasn't in a position where I had to pay back a ton of money, but my bank account, put it this way, was triple zero. I didn't have a safety-, like my parents didn't have any money. There was like no safety net or anything like that.

I grew up in a kind of a raise yourself up by the bootstraps type family. Moving back at home was not an option, let's just say that.

Fortunately, I did pretty well, and going back to the investment thing, I didn't know what I wanted to do, but I was still fascinated with investing. I ended up getting a couple of job offers on Wall Street. One was with the investment bank, Goldman Sachs, and then the other was with the financial services and insurance giant, AIG, American International Group. You'll remember AIG, you know, they were formally on the front of Manchester United's jerseys, as like a sponsor.

Big international company. I worked on Wall Street after university for a couple of years. I realized my passion, the thing that I really wanted to do was I wanted to get back to China. I really wanted to get back to China, do business in China, and so found a way in at AIG where basically convinced them, I said, hey, listen. I speak Chinese, which I do. I've got all this experience. What I want to do is I want to go to China. Send me over and let me run your sales office expansion project. After a lot of training in New York and a lot of back and forth, made it happen.

My wife and I, the whole story behind this which is in the book, which I know we'll talk about, that kind of talks about how none of this almost happened. Long story short, we get to Asia, and we spent about five years in China. I was based in Shanghai, and that's exactly what I was doing. I was running a massive sales office expansion office. I had a team of 24 Chinese people that reported to me. I was living out of hotels, flying across, all through Asia and all throughout China. When I was in my mid-twenties, I had this quarter life crisis.

Nicola: A quarter life crisis!

Ryan: Yeah, I know, right. It's like a midlife crisis. Well, I had this quarter life crisis, Nicola, and I know this is, you hear this from the outside, and it's like oh, whoa is me, what could possibly be wrong? Here's the-, I'll best honest, here's what happened. I mean I had achieved everything that I wanted to achieve, and I was at the, you know, 25, 26 at the time, and I said, this is it? I mean we had a fancy apartment. My wife was actually, it was crazy. I was in Shanghai. My wife was based in Hong Kong, which is about a 2 1/2 hour flight. She was doing, pursuing a PhD at Hong Kong University, and I was doing my job. So we'd see each other like every two weeks traveling. I'd fly into Hong Kong or she'd fly up to Shanghai or whatever. We'd see each other kind of twice a month. It was this crazy bi-country marriage.

I said this is it? This was before we had kids. We had a great life, decent salary. It's as cushy as it sounds. I was making money in US dollars, spending money in Chinese Renminbi, and putting a lot of money into our retirement and everything like that. But it was like, this is it?

I came to a head, Nicola, when I wrote this crazy, spontaneous, twenty page letter to my mom. It was really addressed-, it was really a letter to myself where I basically laid it all out on the line. I said here's the deal. I feel like I have this fire inside of me, and if I don't do something about this now, if I don't do something and take action now, this fire is like a flicker. When you work for a company, whether it's Goldman Sachs, AIG, whatever, the golden handcuffs suck you in.

What happens is over time that fire gets smaller and smaller and smaller. You don't even feel it, but eventually it's just gone, and you're just there for life. Whether or not you're working for one company or ten companies, what I'm talking about is you get sucked into that kind of corporate golden handcuff lifestyle, where you get caught up in all the trappings that you're provided. What happens is you lose that flicker, that flame to ignite and do something. I said, Mom, I don't know what's going to happen, but I want to tell you this. Within six months, I will be quitting my job. I don't know exactly what's going to happen. I don't even have a full plan yet, but I just want to let you know that I haven't lost my mind. I haven't gone crazy. I've got this money-making plan. That's what I called it. The letter, by the way, was something that only two people had ever seen up until about a few months ago. It was just my mom and I. I'd kept this completely quiet. I hadn't even shared it with my wife before.

Super private. I mentioned this to my book editor, my book publisher, excuse me, and he said, let me take a look. I showed him the letter, and he said, this has to get in the book. Every entrepreneur needs to read what you were going through.

Because it's so raw and it's so true. I was at a point where I said I don't know what's going to happen, and long story short, the money-making plan was making money online and building a business online that was location independent and we did. I started moonlighting as an entrepreneur on the nights and weekends. Started studying direct response marketing. I started studying copywriting, I started dabbling with little businesses online. Most of them lost money. Most of them failed.

Nicola: Like we all do in the beginning!

Ryan: Yeah, exactly, and eventually my wife stumbled upon the most random of markets. She was involved in this website called etsy.com. Are you familiar with Etsy?

Nicola: Etsy?

Ryan: Etsy. It's basically like Ebay for handmade goods. A lot of crafters, people who make like handmade crafts sell stuff on this site.

Nicola: Oh, okay, Etsy, Etsy. I've heard of it. I've never seen it, but I've heard of it.

Ryan: Yeah, well this is like back in 2007, I think. In 2007, it was like a brand new thing. She's like hey, Ryan, I stumbled on this site, and here's the thing about this site. Back then with Etsy, you could log in, you could click on someone's shop, like click on their profile just like on Ebay or any of these sites, and it would tell you their sales history. You could see exactly what they were selling each day and how much money they were making each day.

Nicola: Good lord.

Ryan: She stumbled on this one tiny little pocket of that Etsy market which was people selling Scrabble tile jewelry. So jewelry made from like Scrabble tiles like from the game, Scrabble.

She was saying, look at these people! These people are making a thousand dollars a day selling this little jewelry out of their basements. We can do this!

We're thinking, I'm thinking, well, listen, we're in, I'm in China. I have access to all these factories, all this inexpensive labor. I'm going to build a Scrabble tile jewelry empire. I'm going to start exporting Scrabble tile jewelry into the States. We're going to get this stuff in Walmart, right?

Nicola: Oh, it's so bizarre.

Ryan: Then so I take a step back and we kind of go back and forth on this, and I realize, okay, listen, that's not the business I want to run. I don't want to be living in factories in Southern China managing, that's not what I want to do. I want to get out of that type of lifestyle. However, she said, well, what about this? Look at these people here. There were a handful of people, Nicola, they weren't selling the Scrabble tile jewelry, they were selling tutorials. Digital tutorials on how to make the jewelry.

Ryan: We were looking at their sales history and were saying holy smokes. They're making almost as much as the jewelry makers themselves, and this we can do from anywhere in the world. We started going down this path. Initially we had some, we didn't have a lot of success. We made maybe $500 a month, a thousand dollars a month. Eventually we take this thing up to a couple of thousand dollars a month, and then this is 2008, late 2008, things are going well, we're thinking things are going really good, and I don't know if you remember in 2008, this is when the world financial crisis hit.

Nicola: Oh, I remember it very well, yes. That's when I lost my first success.

Ryan: Yeah, exactly. So Bear Sterns went out of business, Lehman Brothers went out of business, and one day I walk into my office at AIG, the Hong Kong new world tower in Shanghai, the 52nd floor. I take the elevator up, talk into my office. My assistant, my secretary has a Wall Street Journal Asia edition on my desk, and I look at the headline, and I, just like in a movie. I grab the thing, I hold it in front of me and I look at the headline, and the headline reads, AIG has filed for bankruptcy.

I look at it, and it was like simultaneous panic and a smile on my face. I call up my wife and I say, honey, go to Wallstreetjournal.com. Take a look at the front page. Tell me what it says. She repeats the headline, and I say, this is the day. I think this is it. This is the day that I predicted in that letter to my mom six months earlier, I would be quitting my job. Little did I know that this would happen. On that day, I turned in, I dropped off a resignation letter that day, signed it, walked it into our CEO's office who was my boss, put it on his desk, and I said this is it. I'll stay as long as you need me to stick around. Two weeks, three weeks, four weeks, whatever, to hand over the transition, but I'm done.

Then I stuck around for two weeks, didn't know what we were going to do next. Sold everything that I owned except for two suitcases, moved in with my wife in Hong Kong. Remember, she's a student at Hong Kong University, pursuing her PhD, tiny little 400 square foot apartment. I went from this big fancy ex-pat fancy lifestyle. We had house servants. We were driven around everywhere, to back to school style tiny little one bedroom apartment, 400 square feet. Only owned 2 suitcases worth of stuff. Sold everything else. I said, I had a $450 laptop. I said all right, honey, I'm going to get to work. I start getting to work, and we're growing the Scrabble tile business, we're growing it, we're growing, we take it all the way up to almost $10,000 a month. I'm thinking to myself, oh, my gosh, we're on our way to building a million dollar business. You know what happened next?

Nicola: I can't imagine. I'm on the edge of my seat though.

Ryan: The Scrabble tile jewelry market crashed.

Nicola: Oh no!

Ryan: Overnight. It was like out of a nightmare. It was like, you know, remember Beanie Babies? And Pods and things like that, it was like the market overnight was so saturated that no one was buying Scrabble tile jewelry anymore. The trickle down effect was that nobody was buying the tutorials how to make it, because no one, it wasn't selling anymore. We had one of these moments all the sudden, like if you look at our income curve and our business, it was like up, up, up, and then cliff.

Nicola: Goll, that's the stupidest thing, isn't it, because you'd think that there was always new kids coming up wanting it.

Ryan: Yeah, well, you'd think so, but it's like these-, it was a huge lesson Nicola, that I learned, which it stuck with me forever which is the importance of not going into fad markets.

I've made a point, every market, we talked, you mentioned the 17 markets that we've generated over a hundred million dollars in sales online since, which you hear this story of the early days and it's crap, how'd he get to a hundred million. Well, I learned a lesson. Only go into evergreen markets. We'll talk about that in a second. Back to the story in Hong Kong, we had this moment where my wife and I looked at each other and we basically said, I won't even, I won't say what we really said, but we said, oh, crap, what are we going to do. We don't have the safety net of my six figure salary and everything like that. All of our money is tied up, I can't touch it, because it's tied up in stock options and retirement. It's just, it's not touchable. We don't have a lot of money in the bank. My wife says, well, listen, I'll just get a job. I'll get a job.

My wife, her background is in history. She has a degree in history and museum studies. She fortunately got a job as a museum curator in Texas, in the United States, at the Brownsville Historical Association. So she said, awesome, I got this job, and we can do this. We can leave Hong Kong. Let's move back to the States. I'll take the job, and you work on the business. Well, the only problem is the job only paid $36,000 a year. It was barely enough for us to stay alive, to cover our living expenses. No extras. We sell everything that we own again. Now we each have our two suitcases, move back to the States. We have nothing. We have literally nothing but the clothes and a few mementos from our travels in our suitcases. We are starting at Ground Zero.

We moved to Brownsville, Texas. We move in the cheapest apartment that we can find that doesn't have bars on the windows for like $400 a month. We get in the apartment and we have nothing. We open this, this is all true-, you're going to love this. We had to open up a US Bank account for the business, and the prize, like they give you like a free gift when you open up a bank account, right, the free gift was a folding chair. Like a chair that you'd watch a football game, a soccer game on the side of the pitch. Like if you're watching your kids play soccer, like fold it up, that was the prize. My wife negotiated two.

That became our living room furniture. So we had two of those little chairs in the living room.

Nicola: She sounds like an awesome person, I have to say.

Ryan: Oh, she's amazing. I could never have done any of this without her. She's my rock. I owe her so much. Anyway, we had that. We had one car. I'd drive my wife to and from work. We had our empty little apartment with nothing but the two little lawn chairs and a mattress on the floor, and I had a desk that I got for about ten bucks, and my laptop. And I'd work during the days and send and drive her to and from work, and I just busted my butt. Long story short, we took that next business, which I consider to be our quote, unquote first real business, from nothing, zero, to $25,000 a month in 18 months. We repeated it using my same process that we had done twice now in the jewelry market, now in the second market which was in the gardening space. Repeated it again in the memory improvement space, and that's when I realized, we've got something here.

Nicola: We've got a system.

Ryan: We've got a formula. And people then, I started getting more plugged into the online community, and I attended a Mastermind, and at the Mastermind I walked people through how I was doing this, how I was entering these new markets and dominating them very quickly. Someone at the Mastermind had a very wealthy business owner approach me privately, and he said, hey, Ryan, would you ever consider for a sum of money being available for hire so you could do this for my business? It was something that I'd never considered. My plan at that point was I'm going to, I've got, if I have 20 of these half million dollar a year businesses, I've got a ten million dollar a year business and I can retire and I'll be done. All I need to do is launch twenty of these things in just 20 different markets.

He approached me, and I kind of threw out a number which was a number I thought he'd refuse, and basically he said, deal.

Nicola: He snapped your-

Ryan: I said, oh, crap, now I've got to do this. Then long story short, that became our business model. I did it in market after market after market. Did it in the satellite television market, in the fitness market, weight loss market, dog training market, the tennis training market, the golf training market, alkaline health, business funding, and the list goes on.

Nicola: I've got a question-

Ryan: Just basically replicated-

Nicola: I've got a question. I'm sure everyone else thinking this, as well. How did you puzzle it out all out? Did it just seem like crazy, your system. Did it just seem like common sense to you, or were you reading voraciously and taking a bit from here and a bit from there. Because you just seemed to have exploded on the scene completely.

Ryan: Yeah. Well, it came like this. I mean it's like an overnight success that was ten years in the making, right?

Up until very recently, I was the secret guy that people, businesses brought through the back door that didn't, they didn't want anybody to know that this person existed, certainly not their competition, who would come in and do magic. Last year, once I really felt that the system was bullet proof, and it really was just a matter of executing and there were no holes in it, we decided to start teaching the system. Teaching this in the form of a course which you've seen, you've had access to.

Nicola: I was not just a customer, I was on the phone to your assistant, well, on the email to your assistant going open this up quick, and I want to do it this weekend! That, I can't even remember, Ryan, where I first heard about you. It might have been another podcast, because as soon as I heard it, you know, Follow Us has been flavor of the month for the whole year, hasn't it, you know, what with the machine and all that stuff. But your stuff definitely stood out as being very different to me.

Ryan: I tell you what, the reason for the methodology and as unsexy as this is going to sound, it's the truth, is it's the only thing I could make work. I tried to get into other markets, and I tried to do what I affectionately call the one size fits all approach, right, where it's, you've got a squeeze page, you've got a sales letter, and you're trying to sell this thing to the market, and I could never make that work. What I found, and this goes back to the jewelry making market, so we were stuck on making just a few hundred bucks a month, plateaued, and eventually what I did is out of desperation, I just asked people why aren't you buying? I'd send out a people who had signed up for our free stuff but just hadn't bought, and I said, listen, we're trying to, we're doing our best here. We're trying to make this as good as possible, would you just do me a favor. Why have you decided not to invest in one of our programs?

The feedback that came back was overwhelming. The big takeaway for me was we were trying to sell one thing, because we thought we had one market, whereas in reality, there were actually four different markets. So we were selling a tutorial on how to make this Scrabble tile jewelry. What we found was that there were people that wanted to make Scrabble tile jewelry that used fancy origami paper which required one process, people who wanted to make photo jewelry. So photographs, almost like little lockets on a Scrabble tile itself, which required another treatment. Because if you used the same treatment, it causes the photographs to run. The third group were people who wanted to do something similar, but they wanted to use glass tiles, like mosaic glass tiles instead of Scrabble tiles, and the treatment again was different yet again. Then a fourth group of people who said, I've got, they said we've got the methodology down, but now we have all these supplies that we bought, what else can we make? What other craft can we make with all of this Scrabble tile supply.

What we did is I said, okay, take a step back and instead of selling one thing, let's sell four things. Let's ask people a series of questions to figure out what they need help with, and funnel them into one of these four things, and overnight, we went from making hundreds of dollars a month to thousands, and all the way up to almost $10,000 a month at its peak. That's when I realized the secret is segmentation. The secret is asking people questions, figuring out what their situation is, and then funneling them into one of several possible directions.

That was the first point where I realized there's something here. Then when we launched that next business, I took that approach from the start, and that's how we went from nothing to $25,000 a month in 18 months. How we took the next business after that to be even more successful, and really how we've had success in market after market. It was more work, Nicola, but I realized it was the only thing that I could do that actually worked. The reality is I had to do it out of necessity because the easy button just didn't work for me.

Nicola: Yeah. You've simultaneously created so much work for me. I had a great big long, sprawling, multi sequence, Andre Chaperon style, Infuse Yourself sequence, and I've now condensed that into a really nice, tight, tidy segmented Ryan Levesque style sequence. And yes, some of those emails, I mean I actually got-, because I'm British, so we're quite polite.

I actually got quite a shock at the idea, you know, when I read some of them. Not because they were rude or anything, but they are very direct.

Ryan: Yeah, very American.

Nicola: They are working like gangbusters! I'm getting, I mean I've put a survey in right at the beginning, moved all of my lists through a survey, so it's all segmented now, and that do you hate me email, I'm getting, I'm having long conversations with people that would never have replied to anything else. They really do think-

Ryan: Oh wow.

Nicola: And I am really interested, you know, they really-, it's astonishing how the response you get from these things.

Ryan: That's, you can't see my face right now, but I'm grinning from ear to ear, because I'm so happy. It's one of these things that once you implement it and you experience the type of impact that this has on your business for yourself, that's when you start to appreciate the type of power that this has. I mean it really does, that's what has me so excited.

Nicola: Well, you know, I've only scratched the surface. You know, I've just dived into some of the most obvious stuff, but the other thing is, it totally gets around this issue of people, you know, you going into people's promotions folders, because the minute you start having a conversation with someone, hotmail and Gmail and everyone thinks, oh, I mean put it straight in the primary one, it's someone they know. It's helping with that enormously, as well. It's brilliant. I can't recommend it highly enough.

Tell us now about, so you're the secret man behind many big company launches and things. How did you end up making your own product?

Ryan: Yeah, well, it was again, like most things in life, it was very much spontaneous. I was approached by someone at yet another Mastermind who basically said, listen, I know you do this for big companies. Would you ever be open to sharing your methodology in a training program. If you would, I would love to put you on as a featured speaker at our event. Again, sort of very reluctant. My biggest reluctance was do I want to reveal my secret family recipe, right? Do I want the world to know this, or do I want to keep it to myself. I was torn for a very long time about that. I said, well, you know what, here's what happened.

2012 I almost, I actually almost died. So 2012, my oldest son was born in February, and shortly after he was born, I started getting sick. Initially I was just very tired all of the time, and my wife gave me a bunch of crap and we just thought, oh, you're a new dad, you're not sleeping-

Nicola: And she was going, you're getting much more sleep than I am, so buck up, lad.

Ryan: Why are you tired, here I am, she's awesome. I mean she's amazing. Like she, I don't know, she's like the Energizer Bunny. I don't know how she has the energy that she has. But me, like I would put my son, I would bathe him at night, put him to bed, and I would literally have to sit down on the couch without moving, just like a zombie, for 45 minutes.

Nicola: Wow.

Ryan: Just stare at the wall, and just take like it all in. And yes, I was running a fast growing company and, you know, I burned the candle on both ends, but the key was followed by weight loss.

I weigh, right now, about 165 pounds. At my peak, when I'm really lifting weight and really heaviest, I'm about 180. After my son was born, I dropped down to 134 pounds.

But I didn't think anything of it. I thought I'm working really hard, I've got a newborn son, and I'm tired all the time. This other weird thing was happening, we live in Texas, in Austin, and it's hot in the summer, like a hundred degrees, which Celsius, gosh, like 40 something for you guys.

It's hot. And I'm drinking water like it's my job. Like I am going through a 64 ounce bottle, like a liter bottle, and I'm drinking it, and then I'm filling it back up, and I'm drinking it again. Like I am drinking water like it's my job.

Nicola: Oh, that's a lot, isn't it.

Ryan: But I didn't think anything of it. I thought, I'm thirsty because it's hot. Because I'm drinking water all the time, I'm not getting good sleep, because I have to wake up in the middle of the night to go to the bathroom a couple of times. So there's this vicious cycle, and that's keeping me tired because I'm not getting a full night's sleep and so on and so forth. I just told myself this story that it was this vicious cycle. Then my wife, and the reason why I'm telling this story is because it's going to answer your question about how did we decide to, or how did I decide to teach this. And it's important. It's important that people understand this because it's going to make, everything is going to make sense. Because if you're listening to this, the biggest question I would have if I was listening to this right now is you've got this secret formula, it's making you all this money. Why the hell are you even teaching it. Like why aren't you keeping it to yourself. It's going to make sense in a second.

I'm getting really sick, and we don't know what's going on, but I'm not really thinking anything of it. I'm one of these guys that you know I hadn't gone to see the doctor in like ten years.

Just healthy man, I had just turned thirty. I was in really good shape, or I thought was in good shape. I thought all was good. My wife said, listen, we've got a baby now. I want you to apply for life insurance, just in case. In case something happens to you. I said okay, fine, let's do it. I'd put it off for awhile, and I said all right, fine, I'll apply. Life insurance in the United States, I don't know how it is in the UK, but what they do is they send a medical examiner to your house. They do a medical exam, take a little bit of blood, do some lab results, and about two to three weeks, you get the results, and they'll tell you what your life insurance will cost, based on your health level. It's a function of blood pressure and everything like that. I wasn't worried. I thought I was in great shape, ready to go.

I go to this event in New York City. It was actually Click Bank Exchange, which I don't know if you're familiar with Click Bank. So Click Bank Exchange was in New York City in Times Square that year at the Marriott Marquee, and I go to Click Bank Exchange, and I come back, and there's a bunch of mail on my desk at home, and at the top was the letter from the life insurance company. So I open it up, open up the letter, and in like a again, like a movie, big bright red stamp, denied.

I'm thinking who gets denied life insurance? Like you get denied life insurance if you're on dialysis or if you have cancer or you know, and so I'm like oh, this is a mistake. Like I got someone else's letter. I called my life insurance agent, and I said hey, listen, you know, I got this letter. It's a mistake, what's going on? He says, Ryan, I need you to sit down for a minute. He says, listen, it's not a mistake. In fact, I've got your lab results in front of you, and he said, and I remember it, I remember exactly what he said. He said, listen, I'm not a doctor, but your numbers are off the charts. And I can't tell you what to do, but I strongly recommend that you go see a doctor immediately.

He said I'll fax you a copy of the results. They weren't included in the letter for legal privacy reasons. So he faxed me a copy of the results, and I'm looking and I start doing research online. Biggest mistake. Do not, when you get results for lab work, do not start going to Google.

Nicola: That is scary!

Ryan: So I got going to Google, and long story short, my internal organs were shutting down.

Nicola: Oh, my god, you'd never have known.

Ryan: My liver was shutting down, my kidneys were shutting down, my pancreas was not working. I had blood in my urine. I'm freaking out, afraid to tell my wife. I tell my wife late at night after we finally put our son to bed, and I said, here's the deal. She starts panicking and she schedules a doctor's appointment for the next morning. We go to the doctor's and again, I haven't seen the doctor in like ten years. The guy doesn't know me. He looks at me and he goes, you don't look that sick, but let's see those results just in case. Stay here. We'll run the lab results, stat.

He runs the lab results, and he comes out, and he grabs me by the shoulders and he looks me in the eye, and he says, Ryan, you should be in a coma right now. You need to go to the emergency room right now, and you are not driving. So my wife rushed me to the emergency room which was right down the street. It was faster for us to drive than to take an ambulance. Get rushed to the emergency room.

Long story short, we find out, I'm in a state that's known as DKA, which is Diabetic Keto Acidosis, which is something that people die from or slip into a coma. This is how people find out they have juvenile diabetes. Juvenile diabetes, based on the name, as you can imagine, is something you get, you find out that you have when you're a kid. Not when you're 30 years old. I'm not the first 30 year old man in the world to find out he is a juvenile diabetic, but it is rare. It is extremely rare. My doctors have never seen it. There are other cases of it that have happened in the world. It is very rare. Long story short, I'm in the ER. I had to spend over a week in the ICU where I was hooked up to basically life support and a whole bunch of different, they had to pump my body with 25 pounds of electrolytes and fluids.

I had all of this time to sit in the hospital. In the hospital, I kind of had, you know, when you come to terms with your own mortality like that, you start to think about well, I'm not going to be around forever. What's my legacy going to be?

I started to, I took inventory of all of the things that I had going on, and long story short, I said well, what is the thing that I'm uniquely gifted at? What is the thing that I can make a unique contribution to the world in, and really what it came, it was very clear. It was the Ask Formula. It was something that I said this has to get out. This is something that is so powerful, so pivotal, I can't just keep this for myself and 25 businesses who are making hundreds of millions of dollars with this. The world needs to see this. Because this is one of these rare things that simultaneously benefits both businesses but also consumers. You know this, because you've seen it. It's something that, it's a rising tide that raises both ships. I said to myself,

I believe that every home page in the world needs a survey funnel. Needs to use the Ask Formula. If that's going to happen, then I need to make some changes, and I need to make some changes fast.

The first step was to start formulating this process into a training program, and we started training people, as you know, around the world. Put thousands of people through that. I said to myself, if we really want to make a difference, if we really want to get this in as many people's hands as possible, we need to put this in a book. I was advised against it. So many people said are you crazy, Ryan? Like why would you give away your secret family recipe like this? Why would you put it in a book? I said I don't care. I want to get this out. This means more to me. I don't know how much time I have. My life expectancy is much shorter than it was, put it this way, 3 1/2 years ago, before I was diagnosed. I came out of the hospital like a bat out of hell, and I haven't stopped since. I've got a goal that I want to get this book in as many business people's hands as possible to make as much of a difference as possible, and that's the reason why we're here today. I know it's a long story, but I think when you understand where it's coming from, you can appreciate the motivation so much more than oh, this is just another book.

Nicola: Yeah, and also it's a great, a book is a great way to give people an overview and bring them to the place where they're in a better place to purchase the training. It's not just people who are running businesses themselves that need it. It's I've got a small digital agency I do Facebook ads for real world businesses offline. One of my clients is a lawyer, a solicitor, attorney? Attorney you say in America.

She's got something like twelve attorneys working for her. The fact that we can segment the people coming into her funnel and send them off to, you know, it's just going to be so much more targeted and of interest. She's got a great big mailing list, but it's all getting the same stuff.

Ryan: Yep. No, absolutely, and I'm not, you know, let's just be honest here, I'm not an idiot. I recognize that publishing this book is going to create a tremendous amount of demand not only for our training program, but we have an agency that this is what we do all day every day is we build out these file funnels for businesses around the world. I recognize, it's already happened, just from these interviews, our agency is fully booked up.

But here's the thing, I'm never going to be able to reach that goal myself. I would much rather that this get out there in the world than be like the Coca Cola recipe that we keep in a secret vault somewhere that we don't share. I would much rather, because here's the thing, it truly is something that I think can change the way e-commerce is conducted online forever, and I truly believe that someday the way that this process works, this is going to be common place. It's going to be so self evident. Right? In the same way that we discuss a landing page today, what we're talking about as far as this asking of questions and using surveys, it's something that virtually every business is going to be using, and we're almost going to laugh about remember the days when people didn't do this?

Nicola: When everyone got put in the same file, yes.

Ryan: Yeah, because we don't do this in person. If you met me in person, you would never say, hey, Ryan, great to meet you. Let me tell you about my agency and why, what we do with Facebook is the absolute best thing for you. No. You would start by saying Ryan, can you tell me a little bit more about your situation? If you tell me a little bit more about what you're trying to do and kind of what your business is, I'll be able to kind of point you in the best possible option or the best possible direction based on your unique circumstances. We naturally do this in person. But for some reason, we go into like robot mode when we're online, and you've got businesses that just try to jam their solution down their throat, if it doesn't make any sense.

Nicola: I think the other thing is it sounds like a lot of work to set up, and actually, you know, as I said, I joked earlier about you tripling my work load, but the best thing about the internet is you do the work once, and then it just rolls on. You put people in the front, then they get segmented, they get stuff that's of interest to them, and so yes, it's a bit of work to set it up, but my god, it just rolls on forever.

Yeah, well, that Scrabble tile jewelry business, I mentioned it crashed. I still make a couple hundred dollars a month from that, ten years later.

Nicola: I'm surprised you didn't get into loom bands. I'm very interested in loom bands at the moment. Crafts are huge, aren't they, it's quite astonishing!   That is just a brilliant story and brings us right up to date. Let's now find out your tips. Now, if you were talking to a younger Ryan or if you were mentoring someone, say, you know, 17 to 18, what would you, what have you learned about becoming a business person that didn't know before and you'd like to share? Business mind wise.

Ryan: Yeah, it took me a long time to unlearn two things. Unlearn the way we're taught that failure is a bad thing in school, right? Especially when you're, I was a decent student, as you can imagine, going to the school that I went to, and I had a paralyzing fear of failure. Right? I was paralyzed about taking chances. It took me awhile to unlearn that. I would reframe everything, and this is the advice I would give myself, and I actually adopted this advice, and this is one of the things that helped me really catapult my, the success I've been fortunate enough to achieve is by treating everything as an experiment. Instead of something being a failure or a success, everything is an experiment. Everything. Because what happens with an experiment. There's no failure, there's no success. You just learn something. We're going to try this as an experiment, and let's see what the results are. When I shifted my mindset to that, that had a tremendous impact on my thinking. It relieved that fear of failure. In fact, that was the thing that really helped us have that stratospheric success in the early days.

That's the big piece of advice that I would pass along to someone who is 17 or 18 is everything that you do, don't be focused on the short term monetary gain, that'll come. You will achieve that hockey stick growth if you are focused on the truth. If you're focused on running experiment after experiment to get at the truth, if you do that, the money will come. Most people convince themselves of lies and tell themselves the same lies that keep them in the place that they're at, and that creates a ceiling. You'll never break through that ceiling. If you are only fixated on the truth and you have that experiment mindset, that is probably the single biggest mindset piece of advice that I give someone.

Nicola: That's an awesome bit of advice. I remember when I read the book, The Lean Start Up, and realized that not everyone in the world knows that they're going to be a success or how to be a success, but if you could just start with something, start anywhere, and then just do experiments exactly as you said. I love that about split testing, as well. It's always the version that you don't like that wins, isn't it?

Ryan: I've learned and I've learned-, see, here's one of the biggest things, and you'll know this in the book, I talk about this, is the reason why we've had success in all these markets, it's not because of me. It's because of the process. The process is all predicated on walking in with a naïve beginner's mind. I even say that. A beginner's mind is a zen mind. Paraphrase that, the famous quote. If you go in with a naïve mind and an open mind and you're fixated on the truth, not based on what you think you know, which is the biggest mistake that marketers make, if you have that mindset, then you will be successful. It's just a matter of time.

Nicola: What about business marketing? What really, I mean it's probably all been word of mouth for you, hasn't it, but if you had to start again knowing, not knowing, you know, what you know now, where, how would you market a new business?

Ryan: Very simple. Get results. Work for free, work inexpensively, whatever, our entire business, really up until this point, has been based on results. I've, I'm a marketing guy, a marketing company that we've had to do no marketing. Why? Because businesses get such an amazing return working for us, they are compelled, the clients that I work with, they're compelled to tell their friends. If they have a friend in a non competitive industry-

They say, you have to work with this guy. That's all you need. The best clients will come through word of mouth.

Nicola: That's very true. That's how I got started with my ads agency, as well. I just offered to work for anyone I knew based on results basis, and you just get going so much quicker, don't you?

Ryan: Yeah, all you need is, I mean you look at our former website, it was literally my consulting website. Nothing, just a wall of audio testimonials. A hundred different people who just in their own words, on the phone, said the results that they got and what it was like working together. That's it.

Nicola: That's so compelling.

Ryan: That's the page. That's all you need.

Nicola: Yeah, so compelling. So compelling. The book is obviously going to be a marketing channel for you, as well, and you mentioned speaking, and you sound like you'd be a very energetic speaker, indeed. Do ever, I mean obviously you get interviewed on podcasts and things, have you ever thought of having a podcast of your own?

Ryan: It's one of the things that we have in the works.

Nicola: Oh, it's so much fun.

Ryan: That's a really great question. Yeah, we've got it in the works and we're still deciding what the format is going to be. It's something that we're really excited about. You're right. The challenge with traveling is-

And speaking is enjoyable. Traveling is a challenge. We've got two young kids. We've got a 3 year old and a 4 month old, so getting away is tricky and really want to try to be here as much as possible.

Nicola: Of course you do.

Ryan: We put on events, but the events are local here in our hometown of Austin.

Nicola: Well, I think there's quite a few marketers in Austin, Texas, isn't there? It must be a lovely place to live.

Ryan: It's truly a mini Silicon Valley. There's a great tech community, a great start up community, a great internet marketing community. So Austin, Texas-, have you been to Austin?

Nicola: I haven't yet, no, but it's one of the places I want to go.

Ryan: When you make it to the States, definitely look me up. We'll definitely get together. It's a great city. I think you'll love it.

Nicola: I've just come back from the Internet Marketers cruise all around the Caribbean and Miami, which was great fun. Just got over the jet lag. What about your money, Ryan? It sounds like you've had, you know, good earnings, and obviously you, god, you were ten years old reading all of those investment books. I can't quite believe my ears. So you've always had an interest in money and had, it sounds like you've got a healthy abundant aptitude to it as well.

Ryan: Yeah, I'd say that with respect to money, the thing that comes to mind here is this. I have this belief that you can, you have to focus on this dichotomy I'm about to describe. I have this philosophy that money as far as where you invest it either needs to be in something that you have full control over, so reinvesting in yourself, reinvesting in your business, and you watch that, you know, the whole adage of don't keep your eggs all in one basket. To paraphrase Warren Buffet, keep your eggs all in one basket, but watch that basket very carefully. That's the first half.

The second half is taking a portion of your profits and putting it away in well diversified passive investments that you just don't look at and don't touch. Because there will come a time, there will be a day where you are hospitalized in the ICU, and there's a risk that you will never work again. There will come a time where our second son was born almost six weeks premature, and we had gosh, $200,000 hospital bill putting him through the neonatal intensive care unit, because he was medivac'd out of the hospital. Things like that will happen.

My philosophy on money is taking that money, a portion of your profits, putting it in investment accounts that are well diversified. I have this belief system that I'd bet on the overall economy, as a whole, growing over the long term. I don't take specific company bets. Because who knows if Facebook is going to go the way of My Space. I don't know. I'm not smart enough to know that. I don't spend all day every day looking at stock chart patterns or company reports. But I do believe that the overall global economy, as a whole, will grow over time.

So it's a mix of investing in fixed income and equities. It's a mix in investing domestic equities, international. Micro CAP, Small CAP, Mid CAP, and Large CAP. Investing in real estate REITs, so real estate investment vehicles, investing in foreign exchange. Diversified across all asset classes, all geographies and all sizes. When you do that, you put yourself in a position to not have to worry about your money day in and day out, and you know that in the short term, there will be ups and downs, but in the long term, if you bet that the global economy will grow as a whole, you're going to be in good shape.

Nicola: I totally agree, because you know that packet of shares that my ex-husband was left by his aunt had grown enormously. I think it was worth something like, you know, 7,000 pounds when he was left it, but by the time we found it again, 15 years later, it was 46,000 pounds. It was very cool, and we were able to invest that into something that kept us for a long time.

Ryan: Sure.

Nicola: Awesome. So what are you most looking forward to over the next twelve months?

Ryan: I'd say right now it has to be our book. The book is entitled Ask.

Nicola: Ask. It's a lovely cover. Really nice cover.

Ryan: Appreciate that, and we're just so excited. The book is coming out within the next month. We have over 10,000 preorders of the book just in a few weeks. People are really excited about the book. I'm pretty excited about that. We really want to get the book in as many people's hands as possible. The book is, the first third of the book is a little bit of my story and how the Ask Formula came about, which also includes some of the things that we didn't even have a chance to talk about today. Some of the more nuanced-

Nicola: An hour is too short.

Ryan: Yeah. Then the second two thirds of the book is all about the methodology. This is where you actually learn the step by step process for how to apply the Ask Formula in your business. To the point that we raised earlier, we left no stone unturned. What I mean by that is this is not one of these books where it's just a tease, where it's ha, ha, ha, you have to buy our training program to really get the meat, no, I lay it out on the line. It's all there, so you can literally take the book and implement the process in your business. It's not something that I, a decision that I made very lightly, because as you know, we sell our training programs for a very high price. But I wanted to get it out there.

Again, what's more important to me know is that this book gets in as many people's hands as possible, and people use the methodology. To that point, Nicola, I think we have a special arrangement where we'll be able to give away a few physical copies of the book to your listeners as a way of saying thanks.

Nicola: Well, that would be awesome, because I'm a living testimonial for you. I mean just one of the things I did was reactivate a list of 1500 people using your techniques that I'd written off to be honest. That's working great. As I say, my deliverability is up, my response is up. I'm actually having meaningful conversations with my customers and potential future customers. So run, don't walk, to the URL that Ryan is going to give you right now.

Ryan: So the URL is if you go to askformula.com, so that's a-s-k, like the question, ask, formula.com forward slash, Nicola, n-i-c-o-l-a, if you go to that specific page, and then you enter your name and email, and then when you're asked to check out, you'll see a price for the book, pay very close attention. If you enter the coupon code, nicola2015, it'll take the price that you see on that page down to zero. I'll actually pay for your book. I'll even pay for the cost of shipping to ship it to your doorstep. Now we're going to do this, I believe we have 50 books available, so first come first served for anybody who is interested in taking advantage of this opportunity. This opportunity will be available until the book is released at publication. The rules we have with our publisher is we can't give away the book-

Once the book is actually on the market. But before it's released, we, it would be an honor for me to make this available just as a special gift. Really as a way of saying thanks to you, Nicola, for being so generous in helping us spread the message and being such an awesome supporter. And really to everybody who is listening to this right now who would like to learn more about this exciting process and how you might be able to apply it in your business.

Nicola: That's awesome. You know, we've moved a whole, and I'll tell you something, my sister Sara, she doesn't change our schedule around lightly, but because I'm so keen on the whole thing and you know I really wanted to move around to get you in before the book came out. Really, go to that URL quickly, because this podcast now goes out in 89 countries, so those 50 books are going to go like hotcakes. Get there fast! There will be a link underneath the podcast episode on the blog, but I'm pretty sure they're all going to go just from the first fifty people who listen to this. Ryan, it's been an absolute joy. I just want to thank you for being so incredibly open and honest and telling us your story. It's, you nearly moved me to tears on several occasions, so thank you so much for that.

Ryan: Thank you for the opportunity. It's really an honor, and I'm just so thankful that you graciously took time to be with me here today. Thank you so much, and we should do it again some time soon.

Nicola: Well, I'll be revisiting, you know, some of the people on the podcasts for sure, so I, you're top of the list. Thank you very much! Lovely to talk to you, and have a lovely evening.

Ryan: Take care. Bye bye.

Nicola: Bye.

Visit Ryan at AskMethod.com

ABOUT THE AUTHOR

Nicola Cairncross is a successful business author, a podcast host at "Own It! The Podcast" and she loves to mentor business owners to transform their businesses to give them more time, more profits and to better support their dreams.

She does that via her Inner Circle community and a six-week training programme called The Pivot Point. Nicola is previously the owner of a successful Facebook Ads Agency, a training / coaching company "The Money Gym" and a boutique hotel "The Acacia".

She currently lives in The Mani, Greece but originally hails from Sussex, in the UK.

Nicola has been featured in many newspapers and magazines, including Woman & Home (Jan 2007, Duncan Bannatyne's "The Sharp Edge" (Jan 2007), The Times, The Observer, The Mail On Sunday, The Mirror, The Scotsman, RED Magazine (many times), New Woman, Woman & Home (Aug 2006), Cosmopolitan (Feb 2007 and many other times), Elle, Marie Claire, Essentials, Top Sante, Radio 5 Live and CNN Breakfast News Worldwide.

She attends and speaks regularly at events, both on and offline, on Digital Marketing, Facebook Ads, Social Media Marketing & Entrepreneurialism.

On the next page, you'll find details of Nicola's other books.

OTHER BOOKS BY NICOLA

"The Business Success Factory"

We are not taught to be entrepreneurs at school, but, due to these uncertain economic times, many people are starting their own businesses. The failure rate is high and self-taught entrepreneur Nicola Cairncross knows why.

"Traditional advice for start-ups centres around a business plan, whether to incorporate or not, how to order your business cards, all pretty useless when you are just getting going!

I believe that becoming a successful entrepreneur involves "3 Key Business Success Secrets" which include mastering the following

1. Your Business Mind

2. Your Business Marketing

3. Your Business Money

and this book will help you do just that! I'm talking from my own experience of many business failures here (and two notable successes) and to leave no stone unturned for you, I've also interviewed many of my multi-millionaire friends to find out what they consider to be the "Secrets Of Success" in business."

Nicola has brought her inspirational, practical, down to earth style, much praised in her wealth creation book "The Money Gym", to the business of becoming a successful entrepreneur.

If you want to start a lean, agile, extra-profitable business that suits YOUR skills, strengths and lifestyle aspirations then you really can't ignore this book.

"The Money Gym: The Ultimate Wealth Workout (2nd edition)"

Improve your Financial Fitness and Live a Wealthier Life…

Discover how to – quickly and simply – take control, make much more money and create multiple and passive income streams from business, property, the stock-market and the internet.

This new and fully updated second edition of The Money Gym will enable you to earn more, shed toxic debt, keep more of what you earn, tone your financial muscles and come out winning no matter what the financial market is doing.

In this acclaimed 9-step wealth building programme you will learn…

* How to tap into the 4 major sources of financial independence

*How to develop the right money mindset and why it's so important

*Powerful immutable laws of money that work no matter what the market is up to

*How to shed toxic debt and build habits that ensure you never get caught again

*How minding your own business and mastering the internet could be the fastest way to riches

*Tactics to master cash flow control so that you always know where you are with your money

*How to save and invest (and know the difference!) wisely so that your pot grows rather than shrinks

*How to leverage even small funds in order to generate serious investment capital

*Why property, and certain other assets, are still more valuable than savings – even now!

Read this book to discover how to – quickly and simply – take control, make much more money and create multiple and passive income streams from business, property, the stock-market and the internet.

"Finally….a Kiyosaki for the Brits!" Independent Amazon Reviewer

"Read the book several times, and know Nicola from our local Chamber of Commerce. An amazing financial coach whose book has gone a long way to help me get finances on track after several life difficulties and full of great ideas. One note of caution…..you have to do the exercises. If you're too lazy to do them, then chances are you won't get far!!!" Markie Mark, Independent Amazon Review

"How To Market ANY Business Online"

Nicola Cairncross reveals her simple 7 step system of how to market ANY business online. Acknowledged internet marketing expert, Nicola bought her first domain name in 1995 and is using this system today at her digital marketing agency to market clients as diverse as private finance companies, business mentoring, options property specialists, stock-market trading training companies and upmarket introduction agencies.

Previously she's worked online with clients that include a hydroponically grown wheatgrass extract manufacturer, a top scientist creating a groundbreaking cataract eye drop cure for dogs and horses, as well as a wide range of fertility, clutter clearing, career & cement specialists!

So when she says this system works for ANY business, you can see that it does!

You will find this book packed with useful and easy to understand information, with simple effective action steps you can take this week and every week. We KNOW that it will give you the best possible grounding in business marketing and online business marketing in particular.

Nicola covers:

* Why you need to move your existing website to WordPress (or make a new website fast!)

* How to start building a mailing list of exclusive leads you can market to, again and again

* What Twitter is all about, and how you can benefit quickly

* Why Google is going local and mobile; get your website on Page One within a few short weeks

* What Google+ is all about and why you can't afford to ignore it

* How to tap into Facebook traffic and find your customers where they play

Linked In – boring but changing and a rich source of leads for your business

* All about creating a "know, like & trust" relationship with your visitors and customers

* How to automatically follow up and educate your customers about other products they may like

* Leverage, do something once, leverage it across many different platforms to reach new customers

* Outsourcing – it's easy, cheap and done right, builds your business marketing systems fast

Nicola Cairncross is an author, speaker and self-taught entrepreneur who has been making money online and also marketing real world businesses online since 1995, including a house music label, boutique hotel, vintage cafe, a jazz album and an empty room in Mayfair, not to mention her own "The Money Gym" and "The Business Success Factory" books & her "Inner Circle" mentoring programme.

"The Science Of Getting Rich Online"

A recent addition to Nicola's book list is "The Science Of Getting Rich Online".

This is Nicola's "passion project" and sprang to life when Nicola realised that her two teens Phoebe & Nelson were very unlikely to read "The Science Of Getting Rich" in its current format.

She also realised that "The Secret" the book manages to hide quite well within it's archaic language, religion and talk of "formless stuff" was the very thing that most of her mentoring students were missing!

Why did I re-write this classic book "The Science Of Getting Rich" and adapt it for internet entrepreneurs?

After 20 years of making a full time living online, but watching others try and fail, I have been constantly fascinated by what makes the difference between those who make it and those who don't? Is it the tools or tactics they are using? Are there some secrets that only those in the "Inner Circles" know and don't share? Is it the kind of traffic they use?

Having read this classic book (original version by Wallace D. Wattles) right at the beginning of my online journey back in 1998, I really didn't "get it".

But now, after 20 years, when I read it again I realised all the secrets to online success were in here all the time! However, the archaic nature of the language, examples and references made it impenetrable for the modern online entrepreneur.

So my mission to re-write this old classic and make it easier to read and understand started…

FREE GIFTS FOR READERS OF THIS BOOK

If you would like download several free gifts
just visit our website and click the About You links.

Don't forget to download the free App to keep up to date!

NicolaCairncross.com/app

If you would like Nicola to mentor you on how to start an online business OR how to market your existing business better online just visit NicolaCairncross.com and opt in for more info about the "Inner Circle" mentoring programme.

www.ingramcontent.com/pod-product-compliance
Lightning Source LLC
Chambersburg PA
CBHW051652170526
45167CB00001B/433